MW01087398

Parenting the
Highly
Sensitive
Child

"More than a guidebook on Highly Sensitive Children it is a must read for any parent!"

-Lee Carroll

Parenting the
Highly
Sensitive
Child

A Guide for Parents & Caregivers of ADHD, Indigo and Highly Sensitive Children

JULIE B. ROSENSHEIN

Foreword by Lee Carroll:
Author of *The Indigo Children*

BALBOA
PRESS
A DIVISION OF HAY HOUSE

Copyright © 2013 Julie B. Rosenshein.

All rights reserved. No part of this book may be used or reproduced by any means, graphic, electronic, or mechanical, including photocopying, recording, taping or by any information storage retrieval system without the written permission of the publisher except in the case of brief quotations embodied in critical articles and reviews.

Balboa Press books may be ordered through booksellers or by contacting:

Balboa Press
A Division of Hay House
1663 Liberty Drive
Bloomington, IN 47403
www.balboapress.com
1-(877) 407-4847

For privacy and protection names and identifying details have been changed or omitted.

Because of the dynamic nature of the Internet, any web addresses or links contained in this book may have changed since publication and may no longer be valid. The views expressed in this work are solely those of the author and do not necessarily reflect the views of the publisher, and the publisher hereby disclaims any responsibility for them.

The author of this book does not dispense medical advice or prescribe the use of any technique as a form of treatment for physical, emotional, or medical problems without the advice of a physician, either directly or indirectly. The intent of the author is only to offer information of a general nature to help you in your quest for emotional and spiritual well-being. In the event you use any of the information in this book for yourself, which is your constitutional right, the author and the publisher assume no responsibility for your actions.

Any people depicted in stock imagery provided by Thinkstock are models, and such images are being used for illustrative purposes only.
Certain stock imagery © Thinkstock.

Printed in the United States of America

ISBN: 978-1-4525-6692-4 (sc)
ISBN: 978-1-4525-6691-7 (e)

Balboa Press rev. date: 04/10/2013

For my mother, who would be proud of me even though she watches in spirit at this point. Thank you for the wonderful quality of sensitivity. I know we share that together.

For my father who has given me the qualities of perseverance, optimism, and standing on my own two feet. My journey would never have been possible without these important traits.

And most importantly, for the children and families I have worked with and the children everywhere who long to feel at home on this planet. May you have the courage and strength to create the kind of place that finally honors and attends to who you really are and what you really need. Blessings to you.

Table of Contents

Foreword...ix

Introduction xiii

Chapter 1   Confessions of a Highly Sensitive Child 1

Chapter 2   Finding the Point of Connection 7

Chapter 3   The Labels We Give Our Children.................... 13

Chapter 4   Sensitive, Sensitive, Sensitive.......................... 21

Chapter 5   Home Sweet Home 39

Chapter 6   A Good Night's Rest.. 47

Chapter 7   Dealing with The Big Three:
            Anger, Depression, and Anxiety 55

Chapter 8   Education for Wholeness: Right-
            Brain Learning in a Left-Brain World 73

Chapter 9   Parenting Strategies for The Highly
            Sensitive Child 87

Chapter 10 The Spiritual World of the Intuitive Child 103

Chapter 11 The Family System: What We Can
            Learn from the Dolphins 111

Chapter 12 Adult Indigos Coming out of the Closet........... 125

Epilogue: The "Me" Instant Gratification Nation: How
            Society Helps to Create ADHD 131

Foreword

While I was in Japan a few years ago, I was told that this gentle country, so renowned for its collective ways and well-behaved children, had the highest percentage of teenage suicide on earth. It startled me.

I believe that what we are seeing in today's youth is universal. That is to say that it is not something that is caused by a specific culture or specific set of circumstances. My experience worldwide has indicated to me that something very big is happening, and it's happening to all of society. From the children who are strapping on bombs in the Middle East, to the kids bringing assault weapons to their schools in the West, there is a commonality. There is discontent, disassociation, boredom, lack of motivation, and a general feeling of, "Why am I here?" among so many of our children. There is "acting out" and despair—seemingly more each day, if you read the statistics.

There is a thought among sociologists that is a staple: *Human consciousness is static.* That is, it is *what it is* and doesn't change. Therefore, all our social sciences proceed to try and hone in on the best way to deal with what we have decided is a constant set of attributes that is complex but decipherable. The problems are the same today as they were hundreds of years ago. In their minds, we are constantly getting a better grip on what human nature is all about.

What if the sociologists are wrong? I believe they are. What we are seeing worldwide is a shift of consciousness beginning with the births of children for at least the last 15 years and perhaps more. These children are different, and the old paradigm of human nature is not necessarily what we are actually seeing today. Daycare workers all over the world see it first. They tell us that the children react differently than children did 20 years ago. Then there are the schoolteachers and the grandparents (grandparents really are aware that the kids are different!). Then finally, the employers who are starting to deal with young workers who seem to bring an entirely new paradigm of behavior to the workplace. What's going on?

Are all children suddenly "catching" bipolar disorder? Or, perhaps, is ADHD is somehow infecting them all? Laugh if you will, but the statistics would suggest that all this behaves like a communicable disease! It isn't, so something else must be happening.

If we are seeing a change in the way children are, even a small one, then Julie is the one to talk to, for here is a book—an instructional book—that deals with all of this with a fresh approach. Could it be that our society is changing? If so, then what do we do as parents and teachers to enhance an "evolving consciousness"? Do we beat a round peg into a square hole, telling our children that they must "fit" into our society, or do we start to recognize the possibility that we might have a new puzzle on our hands?

It's not a difficult puzzle! If you will concede to the possibility that humans can change how they think and that we may be seeing a difference in basic human nature, then the puzzle starts to be solvable.

Julie knows. She has the experience and is open-minded enough to have seen what many have now acknowledged. In this book she begins to offer suggestions and provide answers to conditions and sensitivities you will indeed recognize in your children. More than answers, she presents a new theory that may very well help thousands of children, right through their parents' willingness to read these pages.

The book is complete. It starts by helping you to understand what is at hand. It walks you through the puzzle and how society actually makes it worse. Answers are all along the way, and perhaps even epiphanies of understanding for those who have so many years ahead of them with small children to raise.

Then it steers a parent right into a big issue: Is it only the child who needs work? Could it be that we can learn something valuable from this new consciousness? More than a workbook on sensitive kids, this is a must-read for any parent!

—Lee Carroll, July 2012: Co-author of
The Indigo Children,
www.indigochild.com

Introduction

In 1991, I found home in a kindergarten class I visited while shadowing my friend Betsy, who taught in the Vermont public school system. That day in January 1991, I understood that I had a connection to pudgy cheeks, dirty, paint-stained hands, dungarees with grass stains, and the way children touch the bottom of my soul.

Now, a little over 20 years later, I realize that although the modalities that I teach and guide children with have changed, children, at the core, have not. What I have seen is that society and its physical environment has an impact on the way we teach, the way we relate, the way we understand, and the way we treat our children. The physical world with all of its toxicities has also done a number on the sensitive systems of the children who are taking in these toxins. I wish I could say that the way we have dealt with these issues and handled some of the changes has evolved.

In fact, I am dismayed at what has transpired.

In 2010, 263 million stimulant prescriptions were given for children under 18 years of age in the United States alone. Really read that number and let it sink in. Two hundred sixty three million American children under 18 years of age (*Fox News*, November, 2010).

Suddenly, it is as if children have all gone haywire or are broken at the seams. Quick, get some thread. Patch them up! We have schedules to keep and a curriculum to finish and soccer practice to get to! Somehow, somewhere along the line children have lost the ability—or the opportunity—to daydream, to play outside, and to wander. And, most of all, to know how to feel *in balance*.

Have more, do more, be more seems to be the modern American phenomenon. Our culture is saturated with it, our schools are infected by it, and our homes cannot be immune to the pressure that so vehemently knocks on their doors. This phenomenon is actually making our children sick physically and emotionally; from the food they ingest, to the toxins they are exposed to at school, to the pace of their day, and the way their homes can sometimes even contribute to their sensory overload.

When I was in kindergarten, I remember Play-Doh, finger-paints, costumes, and cookies. We had naps and shapes and colors and teachers who smiled. We sang songs and had puppet shows.

I will never forget the day while working as a school social worker and went to my first in-service training. It was on early reading intervention, which I assumed was for maybe third- or fourth-grade intervention. Actually, it focused on the kindergarten curriculum and what benchmarks teachers could achieve with their kindergarten classrooms. I was stunned. I actually whispered to the teacher sitting next to me, "Did the principal just say kindergarten? Or did she mean third grade?"

And the teachers' faces at that grade level! They all looked tired and frustrated and sad. Pushed to push their learners, stuck between a rock and a hard place, wanting to be good teachers, but feeling forced to somehow keep up. And then, having to deal with the parents who were already anxious about what reading levels their child was at by the age of 5. The principal pointed back at the SMART Board computer screen. *You see... the percentages of children...blah blah on the standard mean...blah blah of children across the nation...blah blah.* It made my head spin. I had to tune out, or else I might have made a scene at the in-service.

If we could all step back from ourselves and the situation that we have created for our children, I am sure most of us would be in agreement by now. We are all on overload—the teachers, the parents, the schools, the pediatricians, the daycare workers, the social workers, the child psychiatrists, and most of all, *the children.* They are over-stimulated, over-planned, overworked, and over-the-top. They are acting out, shooting out, shouting out, and breaking down. Can we not see that they are anxious, bored, and destructive mostly because they are not really living in a way that supports them and allows them to be healthy and balanced?

Society is not going to change this unless as individuals, one by one, we do. It starts in your own home, your child's third-grade classroom, and with your soccer coach. It starts when you and I decide to get off the treadmill that's moving too fast. It starts by listening to your children and really taking them in. Basking in their uniqueness and following their chubby, imperfect, shy, or messy ways. When you really take in a child, you will see the world in his eyes. Children are wise. They are our teachers. They are naturally sensitive, heroic, and creative. We can learn from them if we do not allow the world to tell us what they should be like.

Why can't a student stand up in the classroom while he or she learns? Why must a kid have *superior* skills? What is so real or important about age appropriateness? Is not emotional sensitivity and intelligence just as important as math skills, standardized test scores, or soccer rank? Do we not honor joy anymore? How many of us even eat dinner around a table with our family and actually talk?

Children are protesting in a low growl and we are not paying enough attention. They are acting out so that we start to notice the ways in which we have gone off course. The numbers of ADHD kids, bipolar kids, anxious kids, kids that cut themselves, pluck out their eyelashes, do drugs, refuse to eat, and are addicted to cell phones, computer games, and media—in elementary school—is astounding. Are we ready to look at the underlying problems and not just label our children and drug them? I hope so.

We are hitting bottom as a society, and hopefully we are seeing that the do-more, be-more, have-more American dream has become a nightmare. We have got to wake up and attend to the delicious souls who need our attention, support, and acceptance just as they are—not as we want them to become or pretend to be. Right now. The time has come for us to stop the madness and sit still enough to discover the magic we have lost.

I have written this book as a guide to help you start to heal your child and your family. If you are reading this, you have probably already tried it "all" and you are still feeling overwhelmed, confused, and desperate to know how to get balance back in your family. We have to unplug from the world that has become so insensitive. We have to start to really care again, give time to things again, and actually pay attention to the sensitivity that today's children and wise souls are trying to show us.

Highly sensitive children are like avatars that can heal us if we are open to their presence. They can teach us that faster, bigger, and brighter is actually not really all that good for us, that amazing things come wrapped in packages that might look different, act different, be messy, or not fit in standard box sizes. Our box has suffocated us and the children who long to breathe, sing, and skip.

Let us peek under these labels and actually find out what causes their inattention. Why is such a child "hyper"? What factors might be contributing to his or her mood swings and rage? Rather than just looking at symptoms, let's dig down to root causes and really attend to the underlying factors at hand.

What we are doing is not working.

This book is a how-to guide for parents that will help to find out what *does* work.

Julie B. Rosenshein
September 25, 2012

Chapter 1

Confessions of a Highly Sensitive Child

As a child I always thought I was dropped off in the wrong family. Perhaps even the wrong planet. Having a highly sensitive heart in this world is hard work. As a child I worried about the pandas at the Bronx Zoo and if they liked the zoo. Actually, I could feel and know what they felt because if I stood still long enough, I could look at a creature or human being and know what they were feeling and sometimes what they were thinking. I know now that I had the gift and curse of clairsentience; knowing and being open to others' feelings even if they are unaware consciously of those feelings themselves.

As a baby, I did not receive much touch or handling because my mother was grieving over the death of her own mother. I came into this world already feeling "needy" somehow, wanting comfort, nurturance, and soothing. As a toddler I was "hyper," enthusiastic, and liked to zoom around the living room moving and pushing furniture, singing loudly, and instigating trouble with my other sisters. One thing they always said about me is that I was "just like her father: stubborn, stubborn, stubborn." When I wanted something I would not be able to let go. I now know that this willfulness was just part of my Indigo personality that had to do things my way.

I had tremendous amounts of energy, enthusiasm, and joy, along with mood swings, sadness, anxiety, depression, and a fierce spirit that came through my eyes and later, my leadership abilities. I never liked following along with others, always had my own way and resented my teachers, elders, and counselors at camp. I wanted to be the one leading everybody! As a young child, I saw myself leading people, teaching people, and speaking in front of large crowds.

I grew up in a Jewish household in an affluent suburb. We had everything materially. I went to a private Jewish day school where we prayed for an hour each day. I loved morning prayers. I still remember the songs and prayers by heart. I had a clear connection with God from a very young age, and would just want to pour my heart out into the songs so God would hear. I had many dreams where I was talking to God or angels and could feel the connection during sleeping and waking hours. My connection at that time was magical and in some ways unhampered. My spark was bright at some times yet very sad at others. Small things affected me on big levels. The energy of people around me really affected my own energy and I calmed myself through eating. I did not like sleepovers at other children's houses because of my sensitivities and anxiousness. I was a born peacemaker, having trouble even knowing where to sit in the school cafeteria for fear of not including everyone or being seen as a member of a friendship "clique." I felt deeply about *everything*.

I wanted "everyone to just get along."

As I grew older and tried to traverse adolescence, my inner pain and unhappiness in life took over and I began looking towards drugs to ease my pain and help me feel connected to something. I was angry and depressed, and drugs seemed to be a way out. I led a double life, going to high school during the day and then getting high on cocaine or pot; staying up all night, watching television, crying, and hoping dawn would come quickly. I remember driving around in my car, wondering whether there were people behind their closed suburban doors laughing at the dinner table or playing ball in their backyards. I wanted to belong somewhere. I felt empty inside. I was looking for "something." I longed for meaning.

This spiritual and emotional quicksand continued until college, when as a freshman my alcoholism and drug addiction nearly killed me. One February evening I passed out in my car, parked at a rest stop, and nearly froze to death. Fortunately, the universe had other plans. At 6 am I heard a knocking on the rear car door, and the knocking continued until I was able to open my eyes. I couldn't feel my hands and feet fully, nor could I move at first—but as the knocking on the door continued, and I had the will to struggle to see who was banging. I clearly heard the words, "Everything okay in there?" I kept wiggling my hands and feet to see if I could start to feel them again. I must have been in the first stages of hypothermia, or close to it—but I finally managed to open the car door to respond to the concerned stranger, only to find that there was no one there. No man. No car. Not even track marks in the snow outside my door.

I do believe to this day that I had been helped by an angel who must have known that my life was about to change. Not all drug-addicted adolescent Indigos or highly sensitive children are as lucky. Some die. Some kill themselves or shoot other kids at school. They shoot up with drugs or shoot out with guns. But I survived, and that day in 1989 was my spiritual and emotional wake-up call, one that in hindsight was necessary for my spiritual path and ultimate connection to my life purpose of helping other children and adolescents that need the kind of guidance that I needed.

How can a sensitive child make it in a less-than-sensitive world? That's what this book is about, and through my own experiences and the many families I have worked with, I have come up with some simple tools and tips that are proven to work both at home and at school. Some tools are best used with the help of a professional, but most are simple enough to be used by a person like you!

I hope these strategies will be useful to you, your child, grandchild, or student.

Note: I will be using the term *Indigo* child throughout this book. I see the Indigo child as a highly sensitive child whose main sensitivity is *spiritual sensitivity*. This kind of child or adult can also be called intuitive, psychic, wise soul, old soul, or clairsentient (picks up on the feelings of people around him or her).

I will also use the term *ADHD*. I see the child who is classified this way as a child or adolescent who also falls into the broader category of highly sensitive child. Most of these children have physical sensitivities such as toxicity, allergies, or nutritional deficiencies that actually *cause* the symptoms of inattention and/or hyperactivity. In most of these cases the hyperactivity or inattention gradually decreases or is eliminated once the underlying causes are eliminated and brought into balance.

Chapter 2

Finding the Point of Connection

In order for us to continue living on this planet peacefully, our society must change. The children of today are here to help us reach this goal. Their purpose in being here is to remind us of what we have forgotten.

Many of us living in this culture are used to distancing or dissociating from our true feelings, the horrors around us, the atrocities of violence, and the chaos of our fast-paced, sometimes meaningless world. It hurts too much. We shop, eat, go to movies, and work too much so we can forget, or stay focused only on our immediate nuclear family.

Authenticity Matters

Most Indigos and highly sensitive children do not want to live in a way that is inauthentic. It is not in their DNA. They refuse to pull the wool over their own eyes and will point out when you try to do it to them or yourselves. They point out and bring forward the things we would rather forget. They don't want to pretend to like subjects in school, the uselessness of materialism and the "social norms" we pretend to like, and the ways our politicians and our government are not truthful. These children are not good at pretending and they are too authentic for it. It would not occur to them to be anything other than what they already are: the truth sayers. Their gift to us lies in their refusal to disconnect from this truth, and they force us to do the same. Most Indigos need to always know *why* because everything matters to them. If you try to ignore their questioning, you will see them erupt in small and large ways, from temper tantrums to school killings. They refuse to be shut down, shut up, or shut out.

As they grow older, they affect all those who come into contact with them. They start first by transforming their families and then they affect the educational institutions, political arenas, medical facilities, and technology-based companies they encounter.

Intuitive Children Have a Distinct Life Purpose

When an Indigo comes to this earth plane, they do so with a very distinct and unique life blueprint that is theirs to bring to the world. Some of these children already start doing their purpose by elementary-school age—the artists, counselors, and healers. Their effect is already known by any who know them by the songs they sing, poems they write, paintings they draw, or the way they will try to heal or help the kid who has fallen off the swing at recess. Other emotionally sensitive children have strong scientific or social interests and then grow these interests into their larger purpose later in life. These children are the engineers, marine biologists, veterinarians, political activists, musicians, and scientists of years to come. And when they come into power, watch out! The world will have to change. They will stand for nothing less. As parents and teachers, we are frustrated by their unyielding stubborn nature, but this is the lynchpin of their power. Their minds have been made up and they will not sway from the reason they were brought here. If we help them follow their interests at a young age, we will be helping them find the inner arrow of their compass. If we force them, nag, or do not accept them for who and what they are, we block their lifeline and key to a meaningful, joyful existence. When their lifeline is blocked and they are not connected to their inner compass, the Indigo child will become sullen, depressed, isolative, and at worst, suicidal. They may turn towards drugs to numb out and disconnect from the world. They may wonder why they have to be here on Earth or may want to "go home," get out, or check out. These children become teens who usually start to smoke pot or use other drugs as a way of making life bearable for themselves.

Many adult Indigos know what this is like too. It is the feeling of waking up in the morning dreading the day because it holds no meaning, no promise, and no joy. As adults though, many of us either chose to ignore the deeper callings of our heart ("I've got a mortgage to pay, and kids to feed!") or we wake up one day in our 30s, 40s or 50s and start over. We realize what we really want to be doing is what is best for us to be doing all along. These are the new business entrepreneurs who have changed careers later in life; they opened up the store they always wanted or start doing healing work they feel connected to instead of ignoring their soul's calling.

Once we and these children are connected and listening to our inner guidance and soul's calling, we all begin to lead a more genuine and fulfilling life. Days become full and fun again. Waking up is not full of dread, but promise.

Finding the Point of Connection

If we give our children the freedom and love to grow in their own likeness and not the image we have for them, we give them the greatest gift: *self-actualization*. Becoming the people they are meant to be. It is *never* too early to help them to do this. It is our job to help them find their *point of connection*–this is the place of passion, interest, and enthusiasm that makes them feel most alive, excited, and connected to life. This is the thing they would want to do instead of most other things, and they lose time doing it. The thing that even though they are labeled ADD, they actually have significant amount of attention for. For some children it is animals, horses, dolphins, nature, theater, or the arts. For others it is building with Legos, taking apart electronic equipment, or inventing on the computer. Know that these gifts and passions are not just "interests," they are keys that unlock their soul's purpose, and the more you can be a detective and supporter of these things, the happier your child will be both at home and at school.

Follow your child's lead and interests. No interest is too weird or unimportant. It is there for a reason. If she loves horses, get her to a horse farm on weekends or after school. If he loves art, have plenty of supplies so he can explore, experiment, and play. Give them the tools or resources to develop their trade or interest early. Enlist an adult to take them on as an apprentice; have them volunteer or enroll them in a class after school. Try to think outside the box in terms of trade schools, home schooling, or internships. Comb your community for continuing education classes, vocational schools, art schools, mentorship programs, and internships that teach in a hands-on way about the subject your child loves. If you cannot find a program that fits your child, you can always start a Meetup group or post something on Craigslist.

It is important to start early and encourage your child's passions and interests. This will lead to having a child that is engaged and connected to the world in a way that matters to her and is meaningful. Once life feels meaningful to a highly sensitive child, the world will begin to look like a place that she wants to participate in and add to. And as a result, she will be able to make a real impact on the world around her that is meaningful and sustaining for her unique personality. It is our job to help these children develop their gifts and then allow their passions to shine forth in the world.

Tips & Tools for
The Point of Connection

✧ Have your child write down his favorite things to do and list which things he would do if he never had to go to school. This list is the treasure map to follow for the next block of time.

✧ Buy magazines and tear out all the words and images that appeal to you and your child. Make a collage and notice where there are things that could be incorporated into her home life or studies at school.

✧ Use his interest as something to work toward as a reward for doing things he dislikes.

✧ Set an example by following your own passions and loving what you do for a living and in your life in general.

✧ When you see your child having a low period, have her take stock of how much time she has been spending on her interests or passions. Help her readjust the balance in her life as needed as soon as possible.

✧ Purchase lessons or hire a mentor for your child in his field of interest. The more time he can spend doing his interest, the happier he will be.

✧ Help her figure out what the next little step (NLS) is. If she loves marine biology and is 11 years old, though she may not be able to be in marine biology school right now, she might be able to volunteer at the local aquarium.

Chapter 3

The Labels We Give Our Children

Is it ADD? ADHD? Oppositional defiant disorder? Is she bipolar? Indigo? Highly sensitive? What label will be next?

D. is a six-year old in kindergarten. He displays strong emotions, tantrums, crying jags, oppositional behavior, and inattention to teacher directions. He has hit classmates, hid under desks, and refused to be a part of circle time. D. was switched from one school to another, and at the second school, they did a thorough psychological and social-emotional intake with parent involvement. The school came up with a working behavioral plan and reward system, encouraging adherence to boundaries, requests, and setting limits with respect to any kind of physical, aggressive behaviors. They also encouraged the child to take "cool down" periods before he got so out of control that negative behaviors surfaced. Within 21 days, this child had gone from three crying episodes to one; he was not

PARENTING THE HIGHLY SENSITIVE CHILD

using physical aggression, and was starting to join in to song circle if he was able to have his choice of seat. He was still quite impulsive and inattentive, but was on his way towards balance in these areas. Things were looking quite positive for this child and his improvements.

The parents called and asked the team working with this child if they had seen improvements within the last seven days. The classroom teacher said, "Hard to say, the improvement has been progressively better in small increments all along." The parent then informed the teacher that the child had been put on Ritalin 7 days ago by the pediatrician who said it would help the child's inattention and impulsivity. Improvements were happening in three weeks of behavioral intervention. Words cannot describe how my heart sank when the team told me this. Not only were our interventions now clouded by a second variable that would confuse our findings, but what would be next for a child put on stimulant before he or she can even speak full sentences?

We are doing a disservice to ourselves and our children if we do not take our time and really find out what the causes of inattention, hyperactivity, and impulsivity are for a child. There are many underlying causes for these symptoms, and if we only look to cure the symptoms, we miss learning where these underlying causes are coming from. We cut down the sick tree without looking at what might be happening to its roots. If you treat the symptom quickly, you actually get rid of the valuable information that informs the future decisions you make for and with a child.

Three months later, this boy was scared when he had done something wrong at school. He was crying inconsolably. "If daddy finds out, he will put me in garbage pail!" As it turns out, this child had been emotionally and maybe physically abused by his father. The roots of his emotional ups and downs and inattention were not as simple as ADD. He was anxious, distracted, and scared for good reason and needed emotional consistency, not just stimulants. Chances are that this child will continue to have attentional problems and that his emotional mood swings will continue to escalate. By first or second grade they will probably take him to his pediatrician and tell him about the continued mood swings and emotionality. He will probably at some point get frustrated in class and hit someone. Then, chances are, he will be labeled bipolar and be given a mood stabilizer to help with the mood swings and emotionality. He will be put on a behavior plan and rewarded for good behavior. He will struggle in school and with paying attention, and as time goes on will probably become more and more agitated or angry. He will probably become angrier and angrier himself and have medication tweaking, along with doctor visits, and maybe try several different kinds of medicines. By around fifth grade he will probably be quite mistrustful of adults and authority in general. He will probably hate doing what he is told and get enraged often. He may even lose his cool and end up in the principal's office often. He will not want to do what his parents tell him, nor his teachers for that matter. At this point he will probably get his last label: oppositional defiant disorder. Then he will start therapy or counseling in school and/or after school. "We just can't seem to manage him. He won't do a thing we say. Always wants to do things his own way," his parents and teachers will say. "Maybe it would be good to consider him for a different kind of school where they can give him more personal attention." And on and on it goes.

In high school and college he may even start to use other kinds of substances to help him numb out or perform tasks. He may misuse his medication or combine it with other types of drugs to help him feel better. He will seek to self-medicate his emotions and feelings of isolation, despair, and failure.

I see kids like this often in my practice. It seems to be the same progression of symptoms and then labels that are applied to that constellation of symptoms. Many schools want to see improvements fast, so the pressure is on to medicate as the first line of defense, not the last.

I get many emails from teens that tell me their stories that sound almost identical to D.'s There are young adults in their 20's who find articles on Indigos and call me asking,

Am I highly sensitive or an Indigo? It sure sounds like me. Do you think that was it from the start? I am not stupid, I am not bad, and I am just different?

And then they may weep on the phone. Their lives suddenly make sense to them in a different way and years of struggle click into place internally.

Be Careful to Know Causes of Symptoms

Just because a child has mood swings it does not mean she is bipolar. Children's moods can be caused by a range of very logical and biochemically based reasons. They may be dealing with emotional issues, suffering from poorly managed anger, thyroid imbalance, nutritional deficiencies, family issues, academic difficulties, or a host of other things. Bipolar disorder is not just mood swings.

To diagnose a child or adolescent with bipolar disorder, there must be at least one period of mania that is manifested by a distinct period of abnormally and persistently elevated, expansive, or irritable mood, lasting at least one week or any duration if hospitalization is required. In addition, during the period of mood disturbance the child or adolescent must experience to a significant degree at least three of the following symptoms (or four if his mood is irritable): inflated self-esteem or grandiosity, decreased need for sleep, pressured speech, flight of ideas or racing thoughts, distractibility, increased goal-directed activity, or excessive involvement in activities with the potential for painful consequences. For a diagnosis of bipolar disorder, these symptoms must also produce marked impairment in functioning and be unaccounted for by other psychiatric disorders due to physiologic effects of substances or medical conditions (American Psychiatric Association, 1994).

Also, just because a child is inattentive does not mean he has ADD. There are many causes of inattention in children. Is her learning style different? Is he bored? Emotionally distracted? Biochemically unbalanced? Dealing with family issues? Having personality conflicts with peers that impede her availability to learn well? Is she an active learner, needing frequent breaks and physical stimulation? Is he eating foods that could contribute, such as colas, color additives, sugar, dairy, or a significant amount of wheat products? Is she sleeping enough during the night? Is he allergic to the environment of their classroom or the lighting in it? Is she experiencing difficulty because she is over stimulated visually?

Also, the symptoms of ADD must be seen across at least two different kinds of settings to be truly diagnosable (meaning at home *and* at school, or when school is in session *and* when school is out during summer months). If your child does not show the same symptoms across these different spectrums, then be careful of this specific label. Sometimes children can be hyperactive when what they really need is proper rest and nutrition. Other times, a child can be inattentive because of the emotional overload he is experiencing both at school and at home. Learning styles can be very different for different children. This is important information that leads to knowing how a child processes academic and sensory input.

Pay attention to what happens when she is learning kinesthetically about things she enjoys. Be aware of what happens during summer months when he is outdoors in natural light and enjoying his activities. There is nothing wrong with a label if it is helpful to gain solutions that work. There is nothing wrong with medication if it is carefully administered after adequate time and evaluation. We need to be careful not to use the medical model to pathologize things that are not problematic but maybe just unfamiliar. We must be careful to never endanger a child's growing spiritual life and gifts because we are unfamiliar or scared of the ways she is different from peers or unmanageable in the classroom. Take your time even though your school system or teacher may have the need to get things under control fast. Once you start the stimulant merry-go-round, it is harder to get off. Medication has helped many children gain the structure and emotional balance to be able to function better in areas of their lives. It can also be a short-term solution while you gain the time and information you need to correct underlying imbalances. Just know that there are many helpful interventions that can be tried before medication. Know that you have many tools that can help to repair your child's situation, not just one.

Tips & Tools for Dealing with The Label Debate

✧ Have your child checked for hormonal, nutritional, or biochemical imbalances to rule out any underlying issues that would cause mood swings, irritability, or inattention in children (such as a thyroid problem, unhealthy magnesium levels, omega 3 fatty acid deficiency, or food allergies).

✧ It may be useful to have a diagnosis so that your child can receive services at school. This can be of utmost importance when helping your child become successful academically and socially.

✧ There are many interventions you can try besides medication to help symptoms of inattention and hyperactivity. It may be useful to exhaust all of these if you are reluctant to use medication.

✧ It can be more difficult to detect depressive disorders and anxiety disorders in children. Work with your health care professional to rule these out.

✧ You can't solve everything at once. Change takes time and if you switch too many things at once in your child's life you will never know what is actually helping.

✧ There is nothing wrong or bad about medication if it is the right medicine for the right problem. Make sure you go to a professional who spends adequate time with you and your child before diagnosing and prescribing.

✧ Do not let anyone force you to medicate your child. Find a professional to help you advocate for you and your family.

Chapter 4

Sensitive, Sensitive, Sensitive…

Finding "Just Right" for Your Child's Sensory System

Sensitive is the key word when you are dealing with an intuitive, ADHD, bipolar, or highly sensitive child. Since their bodies are so much more delicate, they cannot process all of the energy, toxins, and stimuli that are overwhelming to their bodies. More simply put by Gabriella (age 7), "I'm just allergic to the world and my body doesn't like a lot of things here. It's hard just being in my body."

Most of these children have extensive sensitivities that range from food allergies, environmental allergies, sensitive emotional makeup, light sensitivities, temperature sensitivities, tactile sensitivities, and can pick up other people's energy like a radio antenna. Many cannot be too close to electrical appliances, computers, watches, or light bulbs since either they or the appliance experience vibratory warfare.

One teen said:

We go through so many light bulbs in our house that my mom has asked that other people turn the lamps on instead of me. I just make them flicker, pop, and then sizzle. I also can't wear a watch because it never works right, and I try to stand back from cash registers at shops. They always go haywire when I am around!

What does this look like in the world of a young child?

> *Mom, I can't take these shoes, the laces are too light!*
>
> *Can't we get this tag out!*
>
> *I don't want to eat it; it feels weird.*
>
> *I can't shake his hand. I don't want to go near him. His energy is off.*
>
> *I don't want to go to the zoo—how could they do that to animals?*
>
> *I only want to wear my sweat pants; the other ones don't feel good…Why do I have to dress up, it's just a wedding?*

Traits of the Highly Sensitive Child (HSC)

Most HSCs will not want to be inside with fluorescent light and will have mini meltdowns within transition times or large, crowded places. This is common. Their feelings are huge and intense, and if they do not have a way to process these big feelings there will be a backlog which contributes to mood swings, irritability, depression, meltdowns, temper tantrums, anger, insomnia, poor concentration, and low frustration tolerance. Much of the ADD/ADHD we are seeing diagnosed in today's young children is really the discharge or emotional backlog of the highly sensitive child out of balance, and when this type of kid is out of balance, watch out!

> *Life is not easy for us! Because everything matters and we feel everything, our bodies are finicky and high maintenance. We can sometimes be a drag to be around because every little thing affects us from our socks to the atmospheric pressure. It's like I feel like I don't have any skin on sometimes and the world just bombards me with its sounds, smells, and textures. My body gets overloaded and then I just have to blow up. On a good day I get on my bike and pedal real fast with the wind rushing, and that helps, but sometimes I just have to leave the mall or restaurant, or I can have meltdown or blow up. My mom and I can usually tell when it's gonna happen now, so she can help me, and I know what's happening. But it used to be real bad.*
> *(Tim, age 11)*

It is and can be exhausting trying to take care of and be with a highly sensitive child since every detail matters. But it helps when we try to picture or feel what they must feel like in their bodies and have compassion for how hard it is for them. Yes, it's exhausting being a mom when your child has to try on nine pairs of sneakers to find the right one, but how must he feel if he knows and can feel the pain of the man at the deli counter or animal behind bars at the zoo?

In our culture, many have become numb to the pain

and feelings around us because it can be *exhausting* to feel. These kids carry and shoulder much of the consciousness that human beings are distancing themselves from. They sometimes unknowingly shoulder the pain of their families, or even generations of pain before them. Many HSCs feel the pain of the world around them intensely, and when this burden becomes too overwhelming for them, they will numb out with video games, isolation, self-destructive behaviors, or drugs and alcohol so they can just make it through the day.

> *As a child I felt like I was born in a foreign country. I just always felt different and felt everything. I could feel energy intensely from others and knew what kind of a mood my mom was in from how I heard the doorknob turn when she came home, even though I was upstairs in the house. My ears rang frequently with this high-pitched noise. I often had headaches from the energy at school and was nauseous from smells or foods. Tinted glasses helped with the florescent lights that plagued me. I laughed long and hard, but also battled low moods, and feelings of isolation. I forever heard "you are just so sensitive. So sensitive!" Like it was a horrible thing that I had to hide or get over. When I was 18 I started taking pills that helped me to numb out. In one way it felt better, but then I couldn't function at all when I needed to. It was a vicious cycle that I later had to break.*
>
> *(Jamie, age 24)*

Acceptance of the Highly Sensitive Quality is the First Step

One of the most common questions I heard growing up as a child and I still hear from parents of these children is always: "Why is she so sensitive?"

The question is usually asked with a tinge of dismay or failure—as if the child is flawed or beyond help. This only adds to the confusion and challenges a child is already facing. If she already feels out of control and then also feels your shame around the subject, she almost always grows up in hiding, secrecy, or shame—trying to deny, change, or cut off important parts of her.

Simply put, this approach does not work. Your child will need frank and honest conversations with you about how he is feeling and will need you to be on his side in an effort to find solutions. Support is critical for his survival and safety both emotionally and physically. If your child senses your negativity intuitively, you will push him away and have less success working as a team.

Find Support for Yourself as a Parent

A sensitive soul requires an abundance of support, care and gentle bedside manner. If her needs and accommodations frustrate you continually, you will need to find emotional support for yourself so your feelings do not bleed out onto your child. Most parents are usually already running on empty, and if you add in a child with high needs, it can be a recipe for disaster. You must fill your own gas tank so that you do not run out of energy and attention to give. When flying on a plane, the flight attendant will always instruct us to put our mask on first so then we can help our children. You must build on this analogy and know that having your own support and self-energy is of the utmost importance.

Many communities have special-needs parenting support groups or "parents-helping-parents" support systems. Your own therapist or counselor can help you gain the balance and energy needed to show up for your child.

Knowing how to communicate about your child's sensitivities and needs is important for the process of getting help and knowing what will be most effective.

It is very important to zero in on the most significant sensitivities your child has and know which strategies will best help to support, soothe, or eliminate his discomfort. Your job is to help him find the "just right" place as much as you can. If your child is able to find his just right place, his discomfort will be lessened or eliminated. The problem comes in when a child cannot find this place. Most anxieties, tensions, meltdowns, and tantrums happen when your child has to keep it together through his sensitivity zones. This can be hard work, overwhelming, painful, frustrating, and at some points downright intolerable for him. When this kind of discomfort is felt for periods of time without relief, you will need to have your boundaries and some strategies in place to deal with the fallout that follows.

Most children I work with fall into four main categories of sensitivity:

1. **Physical or environmental sensitivity**
2. **Emotional sensitivity**
3. **Spiritual sensitivity**
4. **Social or transition sensitivity**

Identifying your child's largest area of need is important for you and your child. You will want to know what their area of greatest need is and know what strategies will be most helpful in their case. This information will also help you inform your child's teacher, camp counselor, doctor, or therapist.

Characteristics of the physically sensitive child:

❖ Sensitive to sound, noise, crowds, lighting, and electronic equipment; hates tags in clothing, certain textures, the ribbing on socks, and clothing
❖ Needs things "just right" whether it is temperature, texture, or environment; may have tantrum over its "rightness"
❖ Has to be comfortable in clothing and will fight you about certain shoes, collars on shirts, or seams on dresses; prefers velour, cotton, and sweatpants to clothing; prefers slip-on shoes or slippers to any kind of binding shoe
❖ Startles easily, is very sensitive to pain, and usually hates doctor procedures, nail clipping, and haircuts to an extreme
❖ Wants to change clothing quickly if wet, dirty, sandy, or stained
❖ Notices the slightest odor and is very affected by it

❖ Is a fussy eater, having extreme reactions to kinds of foods, the way foods are mixed, or the way a food smells or feels

❖ Very touch sensitive; either craving much touch and deep pressure, or not wanting to be touched at all and will shudder if touched at random

❖ Has problems with sensory processing such as poor balance, touch sensitivity, inability tying shoes or riding bike, and is accident prone

❖ Needs a lot of personal space without other children touching his body, possessions, or workspace

❖ Allergic to cleaning products, rugs, mold, and lawn-care products

❖ Has frequent ear infections, sinus problems, and asthma

❖ Very affected by cleansers, products, soaps, detergents

Characteristics of the emotionally sensitive child:

❖ Very sensitive to moods of people around her, extremely empathetic

❖ Feels things intensely and deeply; can be overwhelmed by these feelings, has mood swings, crying jags, or frequent meltdowns; many times diagnosed with bipolar disorder if depression exists

❖ Can have intense tantrums, angry fits, and be very stubborn

❖ Very sensitive to criticism, blame, shame, or conflict

❖ Usually prefers animals to people and has make-believe friends that he talks to

❖ Usually artistic and creative; can be introverted or socially shy

❖ Needs help with emotional regulation through talking, physical movement, or adult affirmation

❖ Frequently asked why she is so sensitive or what is wrong

❖ Frequently tries to please adults and may prefer to socialize with older people rather than peers his own age

❖ Very intuitive, can know what others need without them verbalizing it, is extremely compassionate to the less fortunate, and will want to save the world in some way

❖ Tends to internalize or personalize things that are not about her; needs a lot of positive reinforcement and encouragement

❖ Notices the details and subtleties of everything including people's feelings, his surroundings, and even the general energy of a place or geographic area.

❖ Hesitant with new environments, people, or places

❖ Picks up on family dynamics, parent's moods, and energy in the house

Characteristics of the spiritually sensitive child:

❖ Has spiritual gifts and tends to be interested in spiritual subjects and meaningful personal pursuits

❖ Can sometimes see auras, angels, deceased loved ones, or fairies at night

❖ Has healing hands, eyes, or words that affect people

❖ Has psychic abilities, is very intuitive, and is tuned in to people's energy

❖ Very stubborn, has anger issues, hates injustice, lying, or manipulation; needs meaning and authenticity in her life

❖ Will tell it like it is, even if that involves being impolite

❖ Has difficulty with authority figures, boundaries, rules, and traditional schooling

❖ Must have people tell him the truth and the reasons for things; cannot tolerate inauthenticity

❖ Has a special bond with nature, crystals, animals, dolphins, or horses

❖ Moves in her own time zone, does not care about time, has a hard time transitioning from one task to another

❖ Wants to change the status quo, the world, and likes to bust through old systems that are outdated; has high ideals

❖ Has strong energy, is a multi-tasker, can be hyperactive; bores easily

❖ Does not want to go to sleep due to night terrors and visions and will want to sleep in your room frequently

❖ Has anger issues, mood swings, frequent meltdowns, depression, and can have suicidal thoughts

❖ Can have problems with drug abuse and addiction in teenage years

Characteristics of the socially or transitionally sensitive child:

❖ Has problems transitioning from one task to another, hard to get ready in the morning and to sleep in the evening

❖ Would rather be in his own world and wants to be alone, with animals, or playing video games rather than be with people

❖ Has social anxiety and problems making and keeping friends

❖ Needs visual schedule to be able to get through school

❖ Tends to want to avoid sleepovers, parties, and social functions

❖ Has a very hard time going to school and coming home from school

❖ Very affected by vacations, change of season, and change in routine

❖ Has poor social-cue recognition or etiquette and does not care to learn

❖ Very hesitant to meet new people and may prefer being with her parent(s)

❖ Has difficulty with school assemblies, joining other children at recess, and feeling comfortable at lunch time

You may find that your child falls into one of these broad categories, although she may have some characteristics from each. No child will have *all* the characteristics of a category, but will usually have many traits of a category as their main sensitivity. Once you find the area of greatest need, you can address each of the specific sensitivities from most acute to least troublesome. Often, it is wise to let some things go as you address the areas of greatest need. Some sensitivities are ones that a child and parent can live with and tolerate, while others must be addressed if the child is going to function effectively in the world around her.

The World of Sensory Integration

One of the most helpful interventions that helps to balance all highly sensitive children is occupational therapy and the strategies that you can learn from these professionals to help your child integrate his sensory system. Occupational therapists have a deep and effective understanding of highly sensitive children. One of the most under-diagnosed dysfunctions is called sensory integration dysfunction. Occupational therapists are currently advocating for this diagnosis to be legally used as a true diagnostic code, but for now, it can be ignored or shunned upon by the traditional medical or mental health fields.

It may be up to you to read up on sensory integration at a local bookstore and find sensory strategies that work to calm your child.

There are also a host of books in your local bookstore and library on the subject. Be your child's advocate to locate OT services for him. Other activities that help to balance the sensory system are:

- ❖ Yoga, tai chi, or karate
- ❖ Bike riding, dancing, horseback riding
- ❖ Crawling, obstacle courses, and trampoline jumping

❖ Hopscotch, Simon Says, running, skipping, hopping, jumping
❖ Nature walks
❖ Playground with good quality swings that can go high
❖ Brain Gym®
❖ Heavy lifting or yard work

The more exercise you can incorporate into your family routine, the better. Leading by example and having fun being active with your children will be much more effective than telling them to "go outside and play." Parent involvement, time, and energy spent doing these kinds of activities will pay off great dividends. You can also check if your insurance will cover occupational therapy sessions. Many times an occupational therapist will be able to also set you up with a home sensory program that can be done in your living room or basement. You can also advocate for school services if your child has an IEP (individualized educational plan) or receives other services during the school day.

Keep a mini trampoline, exercise rubber bands, art supplies, yoga mat, and bicycle easily accessible and encourage those activities over sedentary media and electronics. Most electronics, fluorescent lighting, and computer activities are going to drain or over activate your sensitive child's system. Limit exposure and time spent inside with these activities. Your child will need the outdoors to balance out what her body does when around SMART boards, stuffy classrooms without sunlight, and exposure to toxins such as cleansers, poor lighting, toxic toys which are made from plastic, mold, fast food, toxic paint, toxic air fresheners, scented candles, pesticides from pets and lawns, and carpeting that could upset her system.

If you want to know if your child is reacting to any of these toxins: watch. Observe. Follow your hunches. Did his behavior suddenly change after he ate something? Drank something? Played with a certain toy? Does she feel sick when at school or at home? Did you recently put an air freshener in your car that might be causing him to wheeze or sneeze? A new perfume? Did a lawn company use toxic chemicals on your grass before she played near it?

Since you live with your child, you will be the best detective to notice these things and talk them over with a professional who understands high sensitivities. These practitioners will usually be a naturopath, allergist, or a chiropractor who does muscle testing or kinesiology to find systemic imbalances.

In general, the children I work with respond best to products that are simple and made of things found in the natural world. They also respond the best to after-school activities that are child centered, non-competitive, and interesting to them. Warm baths with Epsom salts will clear their energy, as will exercise and body work such as chiropractic, massage, reiki, and cranial sacral therapy. By far, the best free body balancer is the ocean. Get to water, the beach, a river, or moving body of water. Ocean air has ions in it that naturally restore balance to the body. When your child is having a day when his sensory system is on overload you will usually see hyperactivity, low energy, tantrums, meltdowns, and bursts of anger. He will want to take clothing and shoes off, slam things, punch things, throw himself onto furniture, yell, and kick. You need to recognize when his system is starting to get off balance before a complete breakdown happens, but that may take time. Be gentle with yourself as you observe what does not work and then find out what does. Be creative and listen to your gut. And most of all know that usually your child is not doing these things and having these sensitivities to "get you."

Many times your child will spend all her energy at school to hold it together that she cannot help but break down once she gets home from school and you are with her. Her teacher may not even ever see any of these behaviors because your child will not feel safe enough to show it to her peers. And although it is hard work, you may be her only advocate that truly sees what goes on with her. Do not allow your teacher's unfamiliarity with your child's behaviors sway your knowingness about your child. Trust that your knowledge and observation of what happens is real and needs to be paid attention to.

Also, it is very smart to observe what happens in non-demanding situations such as summer break with no homework or school toxins and vacations in a natural area such as the ocean, mountains, or summer camp. This will give you a truer picture of what is really triggering your child's behaviors. Most parents report that their child is "a different kid" during the summer months or when outside at camp.

If all of this seems daunting, take heart. If you do the leg work early on and find strategies that work, your child will not be unbalanced and uncomfortable forever. In the meantime, try to have as much patience and compassion for his discomfort that you can, while setting boundaries where appropriate. It is not okay for your child to destroy things, hit you, throw things, or damage property. He must know what other things he can do to cool down or get control without making poor choices. Some helpful tools are using a trampoline, crash pad, or Theraputty; punching pillows; running, biking, crying, and swinging; shouting into a cushion; making art; or singing in the shower.

The more you can verbalize the situation for your child and then help her verbalize it, the better. You can say things like:

> *Wow, you must be so angry or frustrated, can you tell me about it?*
>
> *I am happy to help you as soon as you have a calm body and can stop kicking things.*
>
> *I see how much pain you are in. Let's figure this out together!*
>
> *I know you feel badly, but making poor choices is not going to help. What can we do that will?*
>
> *In our house, we do not throw things. You must stop. Now what can we do that is okay to do in this house? How about you trampoline with me?*
>
> *Would you like it if I held you and we rocked together on my lap?*
>
> *I know you are frustrated, and sometimes crunching a pretzel is helpful for you. Shall I get one from the kitchen while you calm down here?*

As time goes on, you will be able to know what works best for your child. So prepare for the worst, hope for the best, and know that in reality, your safety and his safety are the number one priority. Know who your supports are that you can call on for backup. Things will get easier to handle with time. Highly sensitive children do grow past their main sensitivities and become balanced if given the time and support. A good general acronym to keep in mind for both you and your child is HALT—hungry, angry, lonely, and tired. If you or your child is feeling off balance because of one or more of these factors, then take care of that as your first priority no matter what you may have to let go of in your schedule. If you quiet the disturbance first, the rest of what happens will be calmer and easier to take care of.

Chapter 5

Home Sweet Home

The home of a highly sensitive child needs to be a safe haven set apart from the overly stimulating outside world. These children need to be able to have a retreat where they can rest, discharge energy, connect with structure, and find safety.

Many children are in school all day with fluorescent lights, stimulating décor, noise, crowds, and no fresh air. All of these factors lead these sensitive souls to emotional breakdowns and energetic explosions. School is just too much of everything that their systems do not process well. The fluorescent lighting itself takes a toll on their bodies, but then add in all the energy they pick up from the other kids in the classroom and having to sit in uncomfortable desks without sensory breaks, and we have a recipe for academic and personal disaster. It is common sense that guides us to know that much needs to be changed in our schools and educational institutions. Most people thrive when they have natural sunlight, adequate physical movement, times for quiet relaxation, and work for no more than two hours at a time without break. As we know, this is not the situation in many of our mainstream schools and childcare settings, so the highly sensitive child's home must be a place where she can recuperate and recharge her batteries which become overtaxed and drained from her day in the outside world. (Malls, shopping centers, restaurants, video arcades, and movie theaters can have much the same effect on these sensitive souls.) So how can we create a home where she can reset her internal systems? The ideal setting for a sensitive child is really is a space that creates an atmosphere of quietude and relaxation and that has room for play, movement, and creativity. When your child first encounters this serene place, she may be wound-up, hyperactive, shut down, withdrawn, angry, or noisy. This is common, and your home should be the safe haven where your child can get back in balance. How can you create this kind of safe haven?

First of, lighting is very important. Natural sunlight and incandescent lighting are best. Soft light from lamps or recessed ceiling lights are easiest on their systems. Always go for natural light when available. It is best for an Indigo to live in a place where the outdoors is easily accessible. He will need to get outside, ride a bike, go for a walk, bounce on a trampoline, or just run around near trees to maintain his health and vitality. Many of our children today are sedentary and would rather zone out in front of a computer, video game, or television. Set limits around computer time and set a precedent of outdoor exercise time before any other indoor or electrical activities are used. Your child may resist, but stand firm on the fact that he must spend time outdoors before dark. It helps if you are active and physical with him so he sees that you are leading by example. Make outdoor activities a staple on the weekend as a family, and encourage your child to do outdoor exploration, join a sports team, or do martial arts. Your child will be happier and less hyperactive, inattentive, or explosive if outdoor activity is part of his everyday schedule.

Purchase an air purifier or filter for the rooms your child spends most of her time in. Essential oils are also very beneficial to clear the energy of a place (tangerine, orange, and lemon are good for low moods; lavender is best for hyperactivity, especially before bedtime). Proper hydration with good fluids is also necessary. Have your tap water filtered or drink well or quality bottled water. Keep healthy snacks in your kitchen like fresh fruit, cheese sticks, yogurt, or veggies with dip. A fruit smoothie made with protein powder, flax oil, soymilk, and banana can be a very tasty after-school perk-up.

Keep some fitness equipment in the house, such as a mini trampoline, large physio-balls, crash pillows, and jump rope to have handy for rainy days or homework breaks. See what happens if you have your child intersperse movement with homework time (for example, 10 math problems followed by three minutes bouncing on the mini trampoline). Have one room where there is minimal furniture and just pillows or mats on the floor so your child can romp, crash, and jump into pillows. Allow him to set up blanket forts and crawl under things. Make nooks, crannies, and hide-out places for rest, hiding away, stretching, and sensory exercises.

Most children need help with transition times (from school to home, from dinnertime to bedtime, and wake-up to bus time). Help your child develop a routine which she can follow every day so she does not become overwhelmed and scattered. A checklist or pad of sticky notes comes in very handy here. Help her to keep her room and backpack organized with minimal clutter, and avoid overly ornate home decoration. Children function best in places that are *not* decorated in primary colors such as red, dark blue or bright yellow, but rather, pastels and beige tones. This helps to calm and clear their energy. The color of your rugs is also important. I worked with one five-year-old who lived in a house with red carpeting and was chronically angry at home, but fine in other places. When tuning in to the energy of the house, I realized that the rugs and old energy from the previous family were throwing her off balance. Once the family tore up the old carpet from the bedroom and hallways and installed new carpet, the angry outbursts stopped within days. This little girl had been picking up on the energy of the people who were there before, and she was also very over-stimulated by the color red. She is now much happier and enjoys her soft pink bedroom with hardwood floors and area rug.

Organization Helps with Energy Imbalances

Keep the bedroom well organized with objects put away in closets, drawers, or shelves. Too much clutter makes for scattered energy. Keep a large-leaf potted plant by the bed (such as pathos) and limit the amount of electronic devices in the room to a clock or computer behind closed shelving unit. If possible, it is best to have the computer in a different room and have nothing plugged in near the bed. Clear the energy of the room with air purifier, wind chimes, bells, a dream catcher, or clear quartz. Keep soothing, comforting objects in the room that are natural and odorless. Crystals, rocks, stuffed animals, pleasant family photographs, artwork, and favorite music help to make the room comfortable without chaos. Stay away from active, primary colors and stimulating designs that activate the energy system. Keep allergen-free cotton comforters, pillows, and linens. Clean the room often with non-toxic household cleansers and air out the room by opening windows once a week, even in winter. Let your child pick out the kinds of decorating he wants when he is old enough to do so. Children will usually pick the things that are good for their system, or you can gently nudge them towards better choices.

Establish a bedtime ritual which is consistent and enjoyable that does not include television, video games, computer, or stimulating activities. Some ideas would be playing high point/low point, reading, coloring, yoga, Reiki, cuddling, or bath with Epsom salts. Keep sugar or colas to a bare minimum and not consumed anywhere near bedtime. Many sensitive children require less sleep, or consequently, more sleep than their less-sensitive counterparts. It is not unusual for an Indigo to want to stay up late. If he is alert, awake, and well rested the next day, do not have a battle over the late bedtime. Pay attention to what his body needs and help him find balance with it. Insomnia and night terrors are very common amongst younger and older sensitive souls. Usually energy clearing or past-life clearing is needed to help Indigos process past lives, recall memories, or clear out deceased spirits which may visit because they are so "open" spiritually.

Make your home a place of fun, laughter, and exploration.

Remember that children pick up on your energy, so have disagreements with your spouse or family members in private or when your child is not around. Your sensitive child will know when you are angry, depressed, sad, or having conflict. The best policy is to be appropriately honest with your child, taking responsibility for the mood or problem, lest he or she thinks they need to be "the big man of the house" or a "big girl" and solve or carry the burden for you. These are wise children; if they offer counsel, listen to it, appreciate it, and then let them know that you are grateful for their help. Assure them that you are doing what needs to be done to help the situation. Let them be children and do what children do. Let them know that they can relax. If your home is a place of relaxation and comfort for your highly sensitive child, she will almost assuredly be able to use it as a place to de-stress from the overwhelming world outside your home. This will enable her to successfully navigate a less-than-sensitive world, even being in the sensitive body she inhabits.

Tips & Tools for the Home

❖ Limit electronics to outside the bedroom; do not use digital clocks or have anything plugged in near your child's bed. Do not use mirrors on main walls. Mount them inside closets. Mirrors can create energy confusion in a room.

❖ Organize your home in a way that minimizes clutter, with everything stored behind closed shelving units and in closets.

❖ Bring the outside into the inside of your home. Go on a family nature walk and collect a couple of wonderful treasures. Make a nature altar or art project out of your found items.

❖ Use 100% cotton bedding and blankets for bedrooms and cozy places and clear allergens such as dust or mold. Stay away from carpeting, mattresses, and curtains that may need "off gasing," which is harmful.

❖ Find things that are "just right" for your child to sit in, look at, and feel. If she feels good, everyone will be happier.

❖ Find out if your child's bedroom is in a good spot in the house. Are there distracting or noisy things happening next door or downstairs underneath her bedroom? Is the hallway leading to the room clear of confusion or chaos? What are the neighbors like? Is there construction or traffic nearby? Are there people using alcohol or drugs in the area? Sufficient air and light?

✧ What kind of temperature helps her system feel best? Is she sensitive to air conditioners or central air conditioning? Does the oil from boiler bother her? Is she sensitive to the gas stove or ashes/smoke from the chimney?

✧ What does your home smell like? Is there any heavy scent that could be bothering her? Do you use perfume, heavy bath products, or scented candles that are toxic?

✧ Decorate with soothing non-primary colors and wall decor without too much visual stimulation, violence, or depressing mood.

✧ Grow your own food or join a local CSA for the best nutrition and food vitality. Digging in the dirt helps to balance out the body.

✧ Some children are sensitive to the energy of antiques, old heirloom objects, or used furniture. Ask your child if he or she likes the object before putting it in her room.

✧ Purchase toys that are made of natural materials and not plastic. They last longer and are better for the body.

✧ Make sure the wall hangings and music you play in your home has a positive message or visual symbols. These things we live with affect our vibration. Do not keep old, broken things, things you do not use, or dead/ dried flowers. These are energy drains on your home and the children that live there. Make sure your plumbing and water runs smoothly and drains without dripping or clogs.

Chapter 6

A Good Night's Rest

The sleep pattern of a highly sensitive child can be hard for the child and hard for the family he lives with. Quite often your child is not sleeping properly due to a combination of different factors.

The most common ones are:

- ❖ Poor diet, eating the wrong foods
- ❖ Unprocessed energy that needs attention and discharge
- ❖ Lack of soothing bedtime routine or ritual
- ❖ Bedroom energy or layout is off balance
- ❖ Nightmares, night terrors, past-life recall, or night visions

I have addressed the eating habits and home environment in other chapters, but please remember that sugar, colas, artificial sweeteners, and caffeine *will* contribute to or cause insomnia in children. If your child must have one of these substances or foods, please, at least make sure it is two hours before bedtime wind-down. Limit the amount of television, computer, or video games before bedtime. The energy of these activities is very stimulating for their systems and it is optimal to have at least one hour between media time and bedtime. Most of these children are already on energetic overload, and the addition of the electronic stimulus can be the thing standing in the way of their good night's rest.

Daily Routines and Rituals Create Safety and Structure

Many of today's kids do not need quite as much sleep as many of us needed when we were their age since their systems are running on a higher vibration and speed. Notice which days are best for your child and how many hours of sleep he got the night before. Then pick the time and be consistent with it. Give your child a heads up one hour before that set time and use that hour to establish a bedtime ritual that is done each evening (with the exception of special events). The more consistent this schedule is, the easier the bedtime transition will be for your child.

Try to put the time aside to actually be with your child at wind-down time. Perhaps you can write in your own journal as she writes in hers. What better way to set an example than to do it along with your child? Quiet games such as cards, bedroom eye spy, or Uno are great ways to bond without the business of the day getting in the way.

This is a great time to review the day, set mini goals, or visualize for the day ahead. A great game to use is high point/ low point, in which each person tells about the high point, or best part of their day, and low point, or worst part of their day. Ask questions, find out more, and see if there are leftover feelings that can be shared and let go of. Model this for your child by using authentic examples from your own life. Label your feelings so that your child can feel safe to talk and share about his. If your child is not forthcoming, use phrases such as:

> *Well, I bet if I were in that situation, I might feel…*
>
> *Gosh, that sounds frustrating. Was it?*
>
> *You look a little sad, is that one of the feelings you felt when that happened?*
>
> *I remember losing one of my best _____ and I remember feeling very _____.*

No need to solve the problem; just empathize and listen. Then validate any of the feelings that are there. Be gentle. Do not project your own worry onto her. Be supportive without making the problem yours and solving it. Ask her if she wants feedback before you offer any words in response.

Dream catchers, clear quartz crystals, Tibetan bowls or bells, dream boxes, and prayer or wishing bowls are all great things to have in the bedroom. Some kids even sleep with large quartz crystals under their covers or in the bedroom to clear their energy and the energy of the room.

Nighttime Causes Anxiety for Children who "See" Things

One of the most profound and common ways that cause an Indigo sleeplessness is the "things" he sees at night.

Many spiritually sensitive children are so sensitive and open spiritually that they can sense or actually see deceased souls and angels. This can be in the form of shiny lights, auric fields, shadows on walls, outlines of bodies, wavy energy patterns, or hearing voices. Please know that this is a very common attribute that these children possess and that they need not be "examined" or "evaluated." It is not their "foolish imaginings," but a very real and important part of the spirit world that they are tuning into.

If you are able to help him and validate what is going on for him, you will help soothe his fears and to honor the connection he has. He needs mentors, teachers, or spiritual coaches that will assist him in managing the spiritual gifts he has. If you cannot do this, find a healer or teacher who can. This is important and will determine if your child will honor his gifts or push them away and be ashamed of them. The more he understands what it is he is "seeing" (clairvoyance), the less he will be afraid to sleep at night.

It is important to note that angels, fairies, and spirit guides are wonderful companions for our little ones, but if a child is seeing deceased souls that are not comforting or familiar to her, it is imperative that the bedroom and the house be cleared immediately. It is *never* a good idea to have any of this kind of energy around. Those souls need to be sent to the light so they can get on with their healing and learning. They are attracted to the wonderful light they see emanating from the Indigo spirit and are confused as to where they need to be. If your belief system includes angels or archangels, call on them to clear the energy of the place. Bells, chimes, and singing bowls also help to clear the energy of a room. Keep a large potted pathos plant by the bedside table. These plants oxygenate and clear the air in a room as well as attract lovely fairy energies that some Indigos love to talk to and play with. If your child is having nightmares or night terrors, there is a good possibility that he may be having traumatic memories come up from previous lifetimes, or is actually picking up on the vibrational happenings of the planet. This is *very* overloading and scary for his system and will need to be cleared to restore balance to the space.

Past-Life Recall or Night Terrors

I have helped quite a number of children to do a "mini" past life healing by drawing out or telling a very detailed description of what they are seeing at night. Then I encourage them to write or draw a new ending for their story. Just talking about it, telling someone, and knowing what it is can help the child let go of the troubling memories.

One child I worked with kept seeing himself in overalls, looking over a bridge and seeing a child who he did not know in this lifetime fall over the bridge and die. The surroundings were not familiar to him, but the same nightmare happened every time he fell asleep. The memory haunted him most nights and the same awful scenario played out. When we did our past life healing, this Indigo remembered being a farmer's boy and that it was his best friend who died when he fell from the bridge. This child carried years of guilt at not being able to save his best friend from the accident.

We drew out the scenes in vivid detail, but this time, this child re-wrote the ending. Reaching over and pulling his friend back to safety and making it home safely. The night after we did this healing, this boy slept through the night, in his own bed—an occurrence that had not happened for three years. He no longer has any sleep problems.

Tips & Tools for Night Time

✧ Try using a worry box or a dream catcher to help soothe your child's energy.

✧ Limit electronics to one hour a day and stop using them at least one hour prior to bedtime so your child has time to settle her energy.

✧ Epsom salt baths are a wonderful way to clear the chakras and energy system.

✧ Try yoga, Reiki, stretching, meditation, soft music, or visualization in the bedroom until sleep time.

✧ Give at least 30 minutes warning before bedtime preparation so that your child can transition into the bedtime ritual.

✧ Keep the bedtime ritual consistent and timely. Do not debate or argue before bedtime. A child's system becomes agitated and uncomfortable for rest. Just keep the boundary and do not budge or get flustered.

✧ Try massage and deep breathing together before bed. This is the best and most helpful time for touch and connection.

✧ Ask Archangel Michael to clear the energy in the room, and invite him to stay for the evening as your child's permanent watch guard and protector.

✧ Use muted colors on the blankets and sheets (without superheroes or action figures) and limit mirrors, electronics, and chaos near the bed. Put stuffed animals away since sensitive children connect so much with their presence and personalities. This can be stimulating for them.

Chapter 7

Dealing with The Big Three:
Anger, Depression, and Anxiety

Usually, by the time a family seeks help for their child, they have tried all sorts of ways to help their child "get through" the day with all the emotional ups and downs and still do not know how to help their child navigate their emotional world. Most children struggle with what I call The Big Three, which are anger, anxiety, and depression. Some of these children are having daily or weekly meltdowns at school or when they get home from school, and they usually suffer from mood swings between the extreme poles of rage and depression. Some do self-harming behaviors such as eyelash plucking, cutting, burning, or even have suicidal thoughts. Many are not able to complete school days, or become overwhelmed and anxious before they even get to the front doors of the school building. The typical sensitive child has a mixture of emotions he is processing that are partly his own and partly the feelings of the people around him. Some children are even affected by the energy of global events that they can feel internally and intuitively. Since their emotional radar is so sensitive, any number of things can affect these children, including moon cycles, natural disasters, global unrest, and financial difficulties that may be happening at home. Many times I see a child who is given a psychiatric diagnosis but is actually a highly sensitive soul who does not yet have the ability to process all the emotional activity coming in across her radar that is not even her own. A child who is a sponge for other people's feelings will eventually have meltdowns, mood swings, tantrums, hyperactivity, and inattention to try to cope with the extra emotional baggage she is carrying. When the child can be helped to process the energy and feelings, he clears his emotional antenna and is free to receive clear signals, not ones that are static-filled and muffled. As a parent or teacher, you will need to learn how to help your child "clear her antenna." So just how can we do this?

Let's start with the first of The Big Three.

Anger

Most intuitive children come into this world already feeling the disappointment and anger of being pulled from their once amniotic and blissful state in their mother's womb. They like being in connection and whole, and they feel quite a shock at coming into this less-than-peaceful existence here on Earth. They come out of the womb already boxing, ready to take on the challenges of the world. Their souls' blueprints carry lifetimes of spiritual challenge, and they are usually aghast at the way Earth functions as a planet. Of course at birth, they cannot verbalize these things, so they are carrying frustration and rage that needs clearing and healing that even *they* might not know about.

L., a kindergartener, felt that she was born into the wrong family and wanted her "old family" back. She was sure she belonged somewhere else and wanted to leave. She was always angry, stomping around the house yelling, crying, breaking things and furniture, and constantly telling her mother and father, "You are not really my parents, I want my parents!"

When I got the call from the mother of this six-year-old, she was at the end of her rope and did not know what to do. I came to meet the child at their home. I immediately picked up from her energy and the drawings she made that this child had been dragging old memories from a previous lifetime into this one. After some sessions together, I was able to find out what her "other" family was like and what happened in that household. What this child remembers was that they were always under attack, or having to defend themselves with guns and fighting during some kind of wartime.

After talking, drawing, role playing, and some hands-on healing, this child was able to process the old anger and control issues brought with her from that time. She stopped having fights with other kids in her class, was able to feel "at home" with her parents and her house. She made two very large drawings: one of her old family and one of her current one. Both were framed and hung in the playroom. At our last visit together L. pointed to the drawing of her current family and said to her mother, "Mom, I really like you and dad, can we stay together here and have fun?" Her mother smiled with watery eyes and said she would like nothing more than that.

Some children have anger and frustration at just having to do things in school and at home that they really dislike. Most of these strong-willed souls will not want to listen to authority, will balk at boundaries and rules, and will very often hate school since they cannot do things their way and on their time frames. This lack of freedom and having to adhere to set rules will fuel an ongoing simmering anger that is almost always present. It is as if they are on slow boil with little bubbles forming until some event triggers them to actually explode or implode. They will always want to do things their way and feel very frustrated and angry that the people around them cannot think outside of the box the way that they do. Their ongoing anger and feeling of being misunderstood, not listened to, and "ordered around" will be quite hard on an ongoing basis if they are not helped to process their frustrations and learn how to tolerate their big feelings of distaste.

So whether the anger is "old" or current for the child, processing the energy or feelings are of paramount importance. There are some techniques that are recommended for this purpose. Some you may feel comfortable doing with your child, others may be better to do with the help of a professional. You will know what is best for your own case.

Drawing, costumed play, make-believe, or "play therapy" all help a child to access his inner emotional landscape. If the child is young, encourage him to draw what he is feeling or write in a journal. Martial arts, tae-bo, fencing, wilderness adventure programs, climbing trees, punching pillows, and talking to stuffed animals all help to discharge and process the energy that needs to leave the body and energy field. If the anger does not have a chance to be processed, it stores up in a sort of "slush fund" that erupts and overflows in small and big ways, from meltdowns and tantrums to school shootings and oppositional behaviors. This anger, when turned into rage, damages the system, and if it is then turned inward becomes the basis for self-harming behaviors (pulling hair, eyelashes, cutting oneself, inappropriate piercing or tattoos) or clinical depression. Most anger and rage, if not discharged, just turns inward and can immobilize the child with feelings of powerlessness, despair, and ultimately suicidal thoughts or fantasies.

Do not wait until frustration builds, turning into larger amounts of anger or rage. Clinical social workers, sports coaches, favorite teachers or mentors, family members, or martial-arts teachers can all be instrumental in helping your child or teen. She may need to talk to someone who is non-judgmental, a good role model, and can point her to solutions. Try to help your child find supports that will enable her to keep discharging and processing the big feelings. Most of all, help her to be heard. Sometimes it is our first instinct to try to get a child to just do what you want her to do in an authoritarian way without taking the time to really hear what is bothering her. You will get a better outcome with your request if you allow your child to at least vent first; you validate what the feeling is and then move back to the request. This is a most important task so that the angry feelings do not get acted out in destructive and harmful ways.

Strategies for Dealing with Anger

These strategies do not replace proper mental health support from a therapist or counselor when needed.

❖ **Allow for as much choice as possible.** These children are at their best if they have a say in their lives and future. If they do not have a chance to participate in their own welfare, they become enraged and frustrated. They do not want to feel powerless.

❖ **Make a place in your home for processing and decompressing.** Your child will need a place to come home and "crash" from his day. Make a place in the house with pillows, old mattress, blankets for fort building, and maybe even an enclosed cubby or cardboard box for him to curl up in and block out the stimuli of the world. This helps his body get back into balance. Let him romp, crash onto pillows, scream, write in a journal, be silent, or just hold him.

❖ **Help her to choose from some of these activities:** journaling, drawing, hitting pillows, jumping, crying, using punching bag, beating a drum, doing martial arts, kicking a ball, receiving Reiki or deep pressure massage, swinging, doing yoga, drawing his feelings with color, weight lifting, going into the woods, talking about it, jumping on a trampoline, creating poetry, and singing.

❖ **Find out what led to his meltdown or frustration.** The problem probably started on the top of the hill way

DEALING WITH THE BIG THREE: ANGER, DEPRESSION, AND ANXIETY

before it became a large, out-of-control snowball. Be a detective and find the causes that led up to the crash.

❖ **Look for underlying clinical depression.** Depression looks very different in children and teens than it does in adults. And boys show it differently than girls. If a child is suffering from depression, it can be masked by anger, hyperactivity, lethargy or indifference to life. See a qualified mental health professional for help.

❖ **Be a detective.** Keep a journal or chart that tracks your child's days, moods, meltdowns, and frustration levels. If you can eliminate the triggers for her mood swing, you spare her the agony of having all the ups and downs of her emotions.

❖ **Relax.** Your child will be picking up on all of your moods, too. The more balanced you can be, the better off he will be too. If you need your own emotional space, explain that to him and tell him what you are feeling honestly. He will intuitively know, so you might as well model good ways of dealing appropriately with your feelings. You cannot expect your Indigo to do anything that you do not practice yourself, so practice what you suggest to them. He needs your emotional consistency, availability, and structure to feel safe in his own skin.

Depression

Most of the calls I get from parents and grandparents are about children or teens that cannot cope with the world around them and start refusing to go to school.

One grandmother had called me and said:

> *Most of the time he just wants to watch TV or stay in the basement with video games and the Internet. The only thing that interests him is his art, and when he draws, he actually looks awake and focuses, but other than that, he would rather sleep. He refuses to get dressed or go to school. I cannot force him to go to school anymore because I cannot physically lift him, and the principal is ready to call DCF or maybe the police. We did the homeschooling thing for one month, but just even getting him out of bed was a major task. Neither one of us wants him to go back on those awful medications that gave him headaches and insomnia, but if something doesn't change, I may have to send him away.*

Another call was from a concerned mother:

> *She started shooting up with the medicine she found at her job at the veterinarian's office. They use it on cats, and she was getting high off of it. She promised that she wasn't smoking pot anymore…but I found seeds in her drawer. The veterinarian job was the best job she has had, but now they are going to fire her because she stole the drugs and got high. She will not*

go to school, and that job was the only thing she seemed to want to wake up for. Now I have to call the police when she cuts school and stays out at night. I frankly have no idea what to do anymore.

After talking and working with the family of this adolescent, it turns out that the 16-year-old is a budding marine biologist and animal healer. Her vibration attracts dolphins when she surfs, and her life dream is to learn about and work with autistic children and dolphins. School and indoors away from the water were the problem; more water time was the answer. We helped her train and apply for an internship at the local aquarium, made extra time for her surfing, and doubled her weekend trip times to the ocean. She began to want to get out of bed and do things out in the world. She was able "make it" through her school day knowing that she and the dolphins would connect soon enough.

Most sensitive souls suffer from depression, especially if they have unhealed anger issues or are cut off from the things that make their hearts sing. If they are forced to study what does not interest them and have a schedule that revolves around things that are not meaningful for them, they will walk through life with an "existential angst"—always feeling thirsty for that which will water their soil. These children need to be connected to their deepest longings, and it is our job to help them figure out what those longings are and give them the resources to move toward them.

If your child or adolescent is not involved with his point of connection during or after school, it will be hard for him to want to do much of anything. He must have something meaningful to look forward to in order to want to engage with the world. Most tweens and teens already feel like the world is unfair and stupid, but if they have no meaningful anchor to ground them, they will most surely want to just give up or check out.

Evaluate Thoroughly for Clinical Depression

It is important for parents to know what depression is and looks like for children, tweens, and teens. It is best that if you suspect that your child is isolating, withdrawing, having feelings of worthlessness, not wanting to live or refusing to get out of bed that you get a referral for a professional who understands childhood depression and can evaluate accurately. Know that there is a difference between the kind of existential or situational depression that can be solved through behavioral strategies and changes in lifestyle and biochemically based clinical depression that comes from unbalanced brain chemistry. Antidepressant medication is a safe way of creating proper brain chemistry so the child or adolescent can even make the needed or suggested changes for the long run. Finding the appropriate antidepressant medication is an art, not a science, and you will need patience and a good professional to walk through the process with you and your child.

Most parents do not know that there actually is a urine test that some integrative doctors use that will evaluate your child's dopamine, norepinephrine, and serotonin levels. This can help to find the right medication that targets the site in the brain that is low or high. There are also some holistic ways that are less traditional than antidepressants that have fewer side effects. Usually integrative doctors, naturopaths and homeopaths can help you with this.

Pay Attention to any Self-Harming Behaviors or Suicidal Thoughts/Feelings

If your child is engaging in self-harming behaviors such as cutting, piercing, plucking, unusual risk-taking, or expresses feelings of not wanting to live, find a professional to talk to and get support from.

It is unpleasant and hard to get these behaviors out in the open, but it is the only way that your child or teen will be able to stop the behaviors and get the help that is needed.

It is never a good idea to have guns, weapons, heavy machinery, open swimming pools, pills/medications, alcohol, drugs, or cars left out, unlocked, or in any place that your child could gain access to. Be alert to who your child is talking or texting with on the phone or on her computer and know who she is socializing with. Boundaries must be set for the safety that she cannot and will not want to set for herself. Do not be so naïve as to think that your child or teen will make good choices because you taught her to. She will need you to help her stay in protected and safe waters. We cannot control our children, but we can certainly lower the risk of fatal accidents and poor choices by being attentive, alert, and present in our parenting. All too often our parenting becomes compromised because we are too busy or distracted by our world and the technology in it to really see our children, be connected with them, and be aware of what they may be involved with that can harm them.

Time and attention is always helpful for your child even if he wants to push you away. Do not take it personally. Be consistent in your need to let him know by your actions that you are not going to be swayed by his indifference or acting out. Continue to let him know that you are on his side even if he has his boxing gloves out and is approaching the ring. The less emotionality you show, and the more boundaries you stick to, the less he will feel the need to fight you, and he may even begin take his gloves off. Acting out and self-destructive behaviors have messages and unexpressed feelings that are underneath them. Try to listen and find out what your child is trying to say.

Strategies for Depression

These are not to be used instead of professional help when needed.

❖ There are both traditional and holistic ways to help a child's biochemistry. Explore all possibilities.

❖ Some depression and despair is caused by situations. Some depression is caused by biochemical levels in the brain that are out of balance. Do the research to find out which you are dealing with.

❖ Be gentle, watchful, and present with your child. She may feel like nobody loves her and she has no reason to live.

❖ Depression will be significantly more of an issue during adolescence when his hormones are already doing flips. Highly sensitive children are more depressed when they are not connected to their life passions or point of connection.

❖ Depression looks different in boys and girls. Sometimes a low mood can look more like chronic anger—especially in boys.

Anxiety

The anxiety that most highly sensitive children deal with is the general feeling of instability and fear that has engulfed our planet. They are particularly sensitive to media hype, atrocities of the world, and the pressure to excel that has become the norm in our world. They worry more about global warming and recession issues than just spending time happily outdoors playing and connecting with nature. Many sensitive children are also picking up energy of worry from the people that are raising them. They hear, "Don't jump so high, you'll hurt yourself!" or "Don't play outside near the sandbox, we just washed those pants!" or "Think of all dad has to deal with without a job! How can you even ask that we buy you something?"

Your financial situation, marital relationship, or housing issues are really nothing that your child should even hear about in your home. Those are adult issues that should be dealt with at appropriate times in appropriate places. Your child is not your emotional support to help you with your own unresolved conflicts, problems, or relational difficulties. You are the one who supports her and she should never be asked to take sides, be put in the middle, or used as a way of you getting back at your mate. Keep things positive, and when there is a problem, you can acknowledge the feelings you are having without making it your child's responsibility to sort through. The more support you have, the better you will be able to contain your feelings so that your child does not unconsciously pick up on and want to solve them.

Unplug your computer and phone, and stop texting for a period of time each day. If you slow your pace down, you will help model healthy, more mindful behaviors and feelings for your child. When he is encouraged to be in a rush all the time or is on your timeline of rush, rush, rush everywhere, his adrenal systems and emotions are affected.

Taking time to unplug and do nothing is worth the uncomfortability it brings up for people. Try leaving your phone in another room. Sit and listen to rain, take a walk to nowhere, have a sleepover in your living room, and try having some fun. Laughter actually relaxes the body and improves serotonin and endorphin levels. This decreases anxiety and stress.

Let Your Child Be Average or Even Fail at Something

Most parents are afraid to think that their child may be behind on the developmental spectrum or just an "average" student. A society that wants children to be more, do more, and be faster about it creates children who are afraid to try things, fail, and learn how to navigate through new and frustrating situations until mastery. If you help your child know that she is okay no matter what happens in school, or when trying new skills, you will help her to put situations in perspective and be resilient in life when failures happen. Let your child make mistakes or even fail so she can learn from them. If you are so anxious "for" your child that you stop her from exploring the world and doing new things, you actually teach her learned helplessness, and she may lose her courage and persistence muscles to work through situations even when not perfect or easy.

The best help for your worried or anxiety-filled child is to help him talk about his feelings, have a "worry jar," and learn how to take small steps before larger ones. We need to calm our own bodies and minds so we can be good examples for these children and also be a safe model for them as they traverse through tough situations. It is also helpful to keep a positive attitude, keep the news and newspapers to a bare minimum, and use physical activity to calm the body when emotions are running high.

It is always helpful to rehearse situations and role play before transitions and new experiences or schedules. Try to keep a consistent schedule or go over the day before it happens. Routines and rituals create safety and comfort for both children and adults alike. Try to help ease change by preparing ahead of time and breaking tasks down into small steps that are more manageable.

It is useful to talk and put things into perspective both for your child and for yourself by asking the question, "How important is it really?" After validating feelings and taking perspective with your child, it is usually best to get moving physically or just try something for 10 minutes and then 10 more minutes. After the situation passes, try to reflect on it with your child and learn that things work themselves out and mistakes are just learning lessons. This eases the pressure that pushes so many of the youngsters in our world and allows them to be children who have fun and experience joy and curiosity throughout life.

Strategies for Anxiety

These do not replace proper professional help for OCD (obsessive-compulsive disorder) or GAD (generalized anxiety disorder.)

❖ Move, move, move. Exercise helps worry and fears pass.

❖ Do the "What's the Worst Thing that Can Happen?" game where you think about the worst thing that could happen and then come up with a solution to that. This puts things in perspective and lets your child know that she can handle things even if they are difficult.

❖ Go over a time that your child was able to meet that challenge before in his life. Remind your child how even though he felt nervous before, he was able to complete the task and feel proud afterwards.

❖ Stop thinking about the anxiety-filled situation and start thinking about a successful outcome. Concentrate on the solution, not the problem.

❖ Hold your child. Do self-soothing behaviors such as taking a bath, napping, massaging, walking, eating a favorite comfort food, or holding a pet.

❖ Keep a check on your own anxiety. Your intuitive child will pick up on your feelings, so try to feel calm and supportive so she can feed off of that energy.

❖ Set a timer for four minutes. Worry, worry, and worry for those four minutes, and when the bell goes off, force yourselves to move on to other topics or situations.

❖ Know that generalized anxiety disorder has roots in biochemistry. If your child worries about almost everything on a very consistent basis, there may be a chemical imbalance that is taking place. Check with a health care provider.

❖ Strive to have a "media-free home zone" in some part of your house or apartment. News, radio, newspapers, and headlines all contribute to feelings of overwhelm and powerlessness. Shut these termites out!

❖ Get out in nature. Fresh air and natural surroundings almost always has a calming affect on children and adults.

Chapter 8

Education for Wholeness: Right-Brain Learning in a Left-Brain World

It is interesting to me that at the public schools I worked at as the school social worker, my case loads consisted of approximately 80 percent boys. Of these boys I worked with, almost every one of them had acting-out behaviors in their classroom and the lunch room but displayed very few of these same issues during our group therapy, or "lunch bunches." Ninety percent of them were labeled ADH D, with hyperactivity being the main characteristic and teacher complaint. Each one of these boys was on some type of stimulant medication. I saw these elementary-age children every week during the school year in group session and also individually when they were having a hard time keeping it together in class.

The interesting phenomenon I experienced was that I

usually did not observe many acting-out behaviors or see the same kind of inattention or hyperactivity that their teachers did. I would often ask these children why they find it so much easier to make good choices during our meeting times. I heard many versions of the same answers over the time span I did these groups. Some examples of their answers:

You talk to me like I am not doing everything wrong all the time.

You give a break from all of it. We can even walk while we talk. I don't have to stay still. You don't get mad at me when I tap my feet or twist my pencil. Sometimes I come in here and I can just rest my ears.

This room feels calm to me. I can slow down.

I get so bored in class. We always have to do everything the same way. Over and over. I can't even write about the stuff I love writing about! I just have to do something to keep myself staying awake in my seat. That's usually the thing that gets me in all the trouble.

I can't sit still the way everybody else does. I can't figure out what she means in math class. The numbers don't make sense. The whole thing just feels like torture.

My legs feel like they are tired and they feel like I have to run all at the same time. How can I listen to what he says when all I want to do is just escape to the bathroom to make my legs feel better?

I can't do one more thing on paper! I just can't

take all the writing and the sheets of paper and memorizing. Why is it all on these worksheets? I just want to do things the way me and my dad do it. We build everything in the garage together. I am happy then.

My whole day is spent trying to pay attention to stuff that has nothing to do with anything I care about.

I can't take all the noise, the stuff everywhere and on the walls, I have no space, there is this blaring light all the time, I get headaches just being there. I feel tired all the time.

It became obvious to me over time that these boys had some things in common. First off, they all experienced some kind of sensory overload and imbalance whether it be visual, auditory, or kinesthetic. Their systems became overwhelmed by the classroom and lunchroom not because they were inattentive to their surroundings, but actually because they were *overly attentive.* They took in every detail around them in rich and deep ways. This produced an overload, especially in their visual and auditory senses. Once they were on overload, they either had to shut down and daydream or escape and avoid work by trying to get out of the classroom or acting out in various ways. It was amazing to me that a teacher would complain about a child daydreaming or completely tuning out everything around them, but minutes later they would walk in my office and say things like:

Hey, where did the other chair with the wooden

back go that was in the corner? You always have that one on that side.

Why didn't you leave the Legos the way they were last week? One of the three guys is missing.

Did you get a haircut, Miss R.? The bangs are different.

Wasn't there a picture of your dog next to the clock? What happened to it?

What I witnessed was that these kids were not inattentive— they were either overly attentive, which produced overload in situations where they had to take in too much information, or they were *selectively attentive* and paid attention only to the things they were interested in or connected to. It is usually the case with these children that when they are interested in the subject matter they will not only pay attention, but also have a hard time transitioning to something else. It was almost as if they are in hyper-focus and would forget to eat if they were not reminded to stop. They also almost always could be attentive if they were permitted to multi-task, move while they learned, doodle, or do something with their hands or legs.

Sometimes their hyperactivity showed itself through their being overly active, but my experience with these boys was that although they were outwardly hyper in their behaviors, internally they were tired, fatigued, and drained. It was almost as though if I had given them a couch to lie down on in my office, they probably would all have fallen asleep after the initial restlessness. Their bodies and brains needed to be rebooted and, most of the time, they could not accomplish this in the classroom or school atmosphere. In my office, however, I always had soft lighting, pleasant smells, minimal wall hangings, healing sounds (if any), large potted plants, a round table with comfortable chairs that swiveled, and a quiet, non-intrusive tone that allowed their systems to settle energetically. I learned what combination of movement, breathing, game playing, talking, or silence would help to balance them enough so they could reenter the classroom atmosphere regulated and available for learning again.

Another commonality they all shared was that they were active learners who were creative and right-brain dominant. They needed sensory breaks, movement, stretching, and alternate work positions to complete tasks without acting-out behaviors. In my office we sometimes did Brain Gym, yoga postures, basketball, or used Thera-Bands. If they arrived sullen, drained, or shut down to talking with me, we just moved our muscles. As time went on, their gears would shift and they would start engaging with me on subjects that were important to them and needed to be heard and validated. If they arrived at my office closed down to even looking at me, I did not push for eye contact. Rather, I would gently and silently just pull out the box of Legos or the sand tray from underneath my desk and would casually start building things with them. No agenda to get them to engage with me, just allowing them to touch the materials and make what they wanted. Is was as if the gears they attached to the next building block allowed the gears in their brain to shift and work in a balanced way again. They became verbal. They let their guards down. They engaged with me and, consequently, made the first steps to start to engage with the ideas that felt so frustrating and stuck for them to absorb in the classroom.

Many times a week a child was just dropped off at the chair in the office across from the secretary near my office door. It was THE CHAIR. The one kids waited until they could be "talked to" by either the vice principal or the principal.

> *He's disturbing the whole class with his constant calling out, weird sounds, climbing all over his chair and getting up and down a hundred times! I can't get anything done with him in my class. Maybe he should talk to the principal. Frankly, I don't think he's read or comprehended even one page of our book. The writing assignment is due tomorrow and he has produced nothing. All the other kids are on the editing phase already.*

It was usually the same thing again and again: a boy just looking exasperated, defeated, and completely ashamed. And there he was—just plopped on the chair with his book and clipboard—waiting.

At one of the schools where I worked, instead of just letting the child wait while someone found an administrator, I started just quietly motioning over to the child with a come here signal and pulled out a chair for him at my round table in my office.

"Tough day with your writing and reading, huh?" I would say. Most of them could barely pick their heads up.

"Well, I, for one, am glad you are here. I needed a break from my work. What book ya got there?"

"Oh, it's just *Shiloh*. I have to write a whole book review, but I can't get the ideas straight. The teacher kept saying I had to get my first page done, but my mind is just blank and I can't even remember the characters! I read the whole book, really,

I did! But my mind is like scrambled eggs. I can't do anything right. She's right. I am stupid."

And usually either the book or pencil or paper on the clipboard would already have been torn, shredded, dented, or doodled upon, if not practically destroyed.

I always ignored the condition of the kid's materials and just kept chatting with him.

"So what's the book about?" I would say, and then quietly pull out colored pencils from my art bin. As the child talked to me about all the things he knew and remembered, I just made little notes. "Dog, best friends, loyalty...yep...yep." And as he kept talking and telling me all the details he could remember, I would push all the colored pencils his way.

"How about you draw it out?"

Usually, the words were not fully out of my mouth before the child was alert, sitting up, looking through the book for specific pages and beginning to draw. And so it went with these kinds of boys. The pictures were flowing, the captions were happening and sometimes even a book in pictures would emerge.

"Great, now all you have to do is put words to all the wonderful ideas you have told me about and have drawn in your illustrations."

I realized after this same scenario again and again that it was always the creative, right-brain dominant boys that ended up in THE CHAIR time and time again. If they were given a more holistic, visual, or kinesthetic way of communicating their ideas, then their brains unfroze and they began to produce work which lead them to feeling a sense of mastery. These kids were usually artistic, outside-the-box thinkers who were very verbal and had an easier time communicating the main themes in words and pictures rather than chronological order or written detail. They knew more about how characters in the books *felt*, rather than the exact timelines of what the characters *did*. They also always understood the underlying message or main themes of the book. They were holistic thinkers like the many right-brain dominant geniuses of our world. Unfortunately, in our mainstream schools at this time, teachers need to deliver a more linear kind of curriculum that leaves little time or money for kinesthetic, visual, project-based learning that our right-brain thinkers need in order to excel in the classroom.

Intuitive, creative, sensitive children learn best about subjects they care about and that have meaning and purpose for them. Usually regular school is boring and meaningless, so if they can have a say in what they learn, you increase the chances of success. Self-tailored learning programs that are hands-on help them synthesize information better. Most of these children despise textbooks, subjects that have nothing to do with life, and standardized tests.

What works best? Science with hands-on experiments, art, nature, literature that has a meaningful theme, creative writing on preferred topic, wilderness skills, woodworking, engineering, medicine, healing, yoga, animals, marine biology, nonfiction, music without rigid theory, and anything having to do with inventing a new way of doing things makes this kind of learner come alive. Movement is always appreciated because they are so active; trampoline jumping, sensory-integration exercises, and occupational therapy are great ways to integrate learning with body movement. Try letting them do some work they hate or find difficult with the reward of being able to do three minutes on the trampoline to clear their energy after as a break. You will get more effortful work if they have something to look forward to that they care about. Most of these kids learn best outside in the woods, or in nature. Waldorf schools, vocational schools, and wildlife skills schools are the closest models that work for them, along with schools that allow for project-based learning and independent study. The next option is home schooling for the kids who simply cannot take the crowds, noise, sedentary learning styles, or old-style teaching methods.

Break up lessons with sensory breaks, deep breathing, or a game. The extra time spent will be well worth your while. Some rainy day, just turn off the lights and listen to the pitter-patter of the raindrops, or on the first spring day, go out and look for crocuses. Remember that learning is supposed to be enriching and *fun*. A child's soul responds to deep and meaningful subjects. When you are coming from an authentic and personally connected space, they will know this and tune in even more. Be honest about everything, even when you think it may be less appropriate or frowned upon by your senior teachers or administration. Your children are craving this kind of soul connection and tune out when everything is "by the books." If it really interests you, then it will usually interest them! And then there's the matter of standardized testing in each state. Sigh. No Child Left Behind. Sigh. A whole book could be written about this very topic and the pickle we have gotten ourselves into. It takes a strong sense of self and connection to your professional and personal philosophy to be able to find the right balance between how much time to devote to standard material and testing preparation and how much time to let yourself create the magic in your classroom that you know will envelop your students.

If a teacher can incorporate positive affirmations, deep breathing, movement, and choice into his or her classroom, he or she will have more success. Keep room décor nice but simple with less visual stimulation since this will drain the highly sensitive child. These children take everything in on such a deep level that they notice every visual detail in your room. This creates visual overload and fatigue. Less is more. Quiet is better. Have small spaces a child can go to for silence and alone time for independent reading. They need this to be balanced.

Structure the day so that chaos is kept to a minimum and their day is predictable. Print out the day's schedule so they know what is coming up. Help them through transition times by giving them some kind of job or ritual to do. When a problem arises, speak calmly, honestly, and from your heart. Do not have an authoritarian tone or land in the middle of a power play. You will lose. Listen to their point of view. Explain what and why you need something done, or what the consequence is for behavior that is not appropriate, in a calm tone and in private. Most of these children already feel self conscious and will experience shame very easily and then shut down. The more a teacher can communicate effectively and calmly, listening with empathy, the better. Know when a student is triggering your own issues so that you do not react in a way that adds to their reactivity. If you can monitor your own feelings and get support from a colleague, you will see that your students will be more balanced. If your energy is clear, you will see that the energy in your room is clear too. What you project toward your students will be what the children act out. Most of the time, intuitive children will know and react to what you are feeling whether you know it or not. They will pick up on what you may not even realize you are feeling. They are keen at sensing your frustration with them and they know when you are distant and not fully present; these are the times they will consciously or unconsciously seek your negative attention. If you do not pay attention to your own emotional world, they will hold a mirror up to you for the whole class to feel or see. When you sense you are "off" or are having issues that your students can pick up on, it is better to be appropriately honest than trying to ignore the situation:

Conversations like:

> *Wow! I can see how frustrated you are by this math. And since you keep kicking other students' chairs, everyone is getting a little off course here. I really would like to finish this lesson, and I am feeling frustrated too since other students are stopping my lesson to complain. How about you take a break, get a drink, and after choice time we will go over this part again, just the two of us. Thanks for making a great choice and taking a break.*

This is where the seesaw technique of becoming less reactive as the child is becoming more reactive is very useful. You will also notice that sometimes the emotional temperature of your room is just "off." That is the time for fresh air, music, in-class stretching, or a fun game. This will break the energy that is stagnant or building and you will be able to "reboot" your students and the lesson you are trying to teach.

Get outside as often as possible and turn off fluorescent lighting. Fluorescent lighting causes reading problems, fatigue, depression, hyperactivity, and headaches for children and adults. Use full-spectrum bulbs or large, incandescent lamps. Investigate the wealth of information there is on Waldorf classroom set-up décor. Waldorf schools use no fluorescent lights, specific wall colors, and limit the amount of wall hangings or posters. If you visit a Waldorf school, you will see how this benefits all students. Use aromatherapy in the room or open windows to let in fresh air. Allow for creativity, thinking outside the box, and self-directed learning. Some schools have life-skills classes, social-skills groups, and social action committees that these deep-thinking children will want to participate in. Allow these children to teach you because they have much to offer us and wise ideas for our society. Spread the word around to your school nurse, principal, and special education or counseling department about what highly sensitive or Indigo children are. Encourage parents to read and be informed too. You may be this child's best advocate if the parent is not aware. The educator who is aware and sets the standard in his or her own classroom may be the one to help the schools change from the inside out, one classroom at a time. Teachers are the ones to lead the way.

School Tools & Tips

✧ Try turning off the lights and working with the natural light of the room. Fluorescent light is known to contribute to headaches and reading problems.

✧ Use "Break Cards", yoga, stretching or Brain Gym to keep the energy of your room stimulating but grounded.

✧ Keep a mini trampoline in the back of the room for kids who really need a sensory break and movement. Let them earn sensory time on it when they complete parts of their work.

✧ Let your students stand up or sit/lie on the floor while completing reading or writing assignments. Many kids cannot work well at a desk.

✧ Let your students earn "Independent Project Time" or IPT on Fridays if they are working well during the week. IPT is the time when all your students can learn about the topics and interests they really love and want to study.

✧ Limit visual posters and wall hangings to a bare minimum. These posters can be very visually overloading to the eyes and create fatigue and inattention.

✧ Have your books, supplies and classroom materials organized "like with like" in bins and closed shelves that are marked.

✧ Read about how Waldorf schools organize and decorate their classrooms. Use some of their ideas.

Chapter 9

Parenting Strategies for The Highly Sensitive Child

Stacey was a stay-at-home mom who had all she could handle with her one highly sensitive boy. Her son William had every quirk she could think of. When she came to me she was exasperated.

> It's as if he does these things just to get me....I don't even know how much more I can do for him. I have lost my life trying to find the right shoes and pants and no-seam socks. We can hardly go out without a tantrum or whine or something bugging him! He won't do sports and parties are just too much. Some days he just spins around the kitchen or climbs up and down the ladder of the bunk beds. There are only three foods he will eat which do not include any vegetable. The doctor, dentist, and speech therapy appointments

are like major events. Dressing in the morning just about does me in. One time I carried him into the car without his pants on properly or his shoes because I could not miss one more morning of work due to his shenanigans! What is it about him? Can't he just deal?! He cries all the time and expects me to drop everything and tend to him when I have two other kids. His brother and sister are sick of it too. Not to mention my husband who thinks I should just ignore him and that he will grow just grow out of "it."

Stacey is a parent who wants to have balance in her family but feels like she is at the end of her rope. She, like many other parents, and especially parents of highly sensitive children, is completely overwhelmed and trying just to survive day to day. If her son has a good day, she does, and if he does not, chances are she does not. She is on the same roller coaster that her son is on. This is typical of many parents and is a hard habit to break since usually both parents and their children are sensitive to energy and moods. So where to start with her challenges?

First off, Stacey did not have any resources or support. Most of all, she had no idea what her son even suffered with, let alone how to handle it. She, like many other parents, could not figure out "what went wrong with this child. [Her] other two were NEVER this way!" Stacey needed some basic articles and books on the trait of high sensitivity in children. She had no idea about why her third child was so different from her first two children.

I handed her a questionnaire for her to fill out on her

first visit. She checked off all but two characteristics that probably did not apply because her son was not yet old enough. When she handed it back to me, after seeing all that she had written, I was shocked that no one had ever explained what may have been going on for her son. I handed her a small pamphlet on highly sensitive children with checklists and behavior symptoms. She stared almost blankly at it. At first I thought that maybe I had lost her, but then she finally looked up and spoke.

"This is him! I mean down to the whole sock thing," she exclaimed. She was stunned. "I felt like I was going crazy or that I had just done something wrong with him! There are other kids like this?"

"Yes, many," I responded, "and with the right strategies in place, your child will do more than just survive; he can thrive, given some time and energy in the right ways by you, your husband, and his siblings."

Everyone else in the family walked gingerly around William to try to not set him off in any way. They concentrated all their energies on trying to keep him from overloading. But what the family did not realize is that in trying to help him not lose it, they had lost themselves. Their entire family revolved around this child. Stacey was so worn out and frustrated that the family had not had fun in years. Her son's high sensitivity had become a curse that everyone, including her, resented but lived with. Sarcasm ran high, whispering about "his issues" was common, and it was becoming harder and harder for Stacey to hide her dismay from her son. Their home had become tension-filled and stressful.

Once Stacey understood more about high sensitivity in

children and how her son fell into many of the four main categories, she was able to breathe a little. Knowing that there were names for things that other children experienced was in itself relieving for her. She also had not fully realized just how negative and tension-filled her interchanges had become with her son. Everything had become a battle that she felt she was losing. Most of all, she saw how every time she "lost it" with William, he became sullen, depressed, and teary. He had no joy anymore and even had a hard time looking at her. He may not have known this consciously, but he felt like he was a leper in his own family. His self-esteem was sinking lower and lower as tensions had risen in his family. Schoolwork fell by the wayside since just getting to school in the morning after finding clothing to wear was such an ordeal.

After the initial meeting and talking with his mom, we discussed the first change that needed to occur with her parenting and relationship with William. She needed to start by accepting and supporting him by being supported herself. Stacey made time for her own counseling sessions and also found a parenting group that was starting in a month. She chipped away at her own schedule so that she could make room for her needs and her own emotional support.

Acceptance and Support Boosts Self-Esteem

When a family's general attitude towards one member of the family is strained, it is hard to feel loving and connected to that family member. Stacey had to start modeling better ways of talking to her son and not talking behind his back or blaming him. It was time to become aware of when her tone was shaming or blaming, and instead use neutral tones, kind facial expressions, and gentle language with William, especially in front of the other members of the family. Stacey was urged to vent her frustrations out in our parenting group and with her girl friends rather than with other members of the family or take it out on her son. Once she started this, she was amazed at just how much rage and frustration had accumulated over the years. She also saw that when she vented with her supports, her reactivity with her son lowered and she had more energy and love to deal with everyone—including herself. When William started feeling warmth and positive regard from his mom, his system also relaxed. They were both able to bring their reactivity down. Stacey also realized that her anxiety about her son and his differences had led her to project into the future that he would never be able to function normally, and that he would not be able to "make it" out in the world. This scared her and caused significant amounts of anxiety that she projected onto her husband and children. Once she was able to admit and contain these anxious feelings and stay in the moment, she was able to see William in a better, more positive light. William felt this and started feeling more confident even if he was still uncomfortable with many of his sensitivities. Once Stacey had a vocabulary and reference point for what he was going through, she could help him verbalize and be aware of himself in a less shameful way.

So, instead of William overhearing his mom complain to his dad about the fact that they would need to buy shoes for "him" again, his mom was able to practice with me in session and then say to William:

Hey, buddy, I noticed those sneakers are getting a little worn out. And I know how much you love them because they are your most comfortable pair. What d'ya say we make some time, just you and me, when we can go and try on loads of shoes in the mall? We will even have time for you to do some laps around the store to make positively sure that they feel good. I know how important it is for you to feel good in your sneaks! And if we don't find a really great pair, we don't even have to buy anything! We can just try another time on a Sunday.

Stacey was able to verbalize what we practiced, and this took all the pressure off of them when the subject was talked about. Stacey chose a day that was cleared of any other responsibilities for the whole morning and had the kids go to the park with their dad. She was able to have time with William that was quiet and uninterrupted. She told him that they would be spending the whole morning together and afterwards he could choose to go to the library or bookstore if he had the energy.

On the big day she left plenty of time and when William was finally able to pick, she bought two pairs of the same sneaker (one in a size up) so that it would be a while until they needed to buy sneakers again. He did not have a meltdown. She brought a healthy snack along for the car ride from the mall. William was quite excited that they even had time and energy to go to his favorite non-fiction section of the library where he and Stacey checked out a book on gems and minerals.

Talk to your Child Honestly about How Things Are

In subsequent sessions, Stacey worked with me on how she could approach the subject of high sensitivity with William in ways he could understand. She had to take responsibility for the ways she had misunderstood her child and had been making some mistakes with him regarding her own behavior. She admitted to her son that her own angry and frustrated feelings about the situation made her short tempered and even mean sometimes. She also said that since she felt anxious and scared about what to do, she was not always level headed and able to be the best parent she could be. She said she was sorry that she "blew up" at him and "lost her cool" so often and that she would be changing her behavior. Stacey explained that she did not know what he was really feeling but now that she understood more about what it was like for someone who needs things "just right," she could be more supportive and less frustrated all the time.

William was silent. He looked down. He grabbed one of the pillows on the couch and smooshed his face into it. Stacey did not try to get him to do anything other than what he was doing. After a couple of minutes she asked if he wanted to come out from under his pillow. He peeked out with one eye, and then the other. She gave him time. After a few more moments he spoke:

> *Mommy, I always think I am bad because everything hurts and nothing feels right. And I want to be like Mary and Doug but it is just so hard for me to even feel okay inside. And then it feels even worse*

when everyone is mad at me! And I know I get angry and can't even think right sometimes. I do these things when I feel like I am going to blow up, but I just want to feel better. Sometimes I just feel out of control and I just want to run and jump and smoosh into you or a wall or even daddy!

Stacey explained to him that they both would be learning ways that they could feel less angry and more "just right." She also said that they would be having a family meeting on Sunday so that Mary and Doug and daddy would understand better too. Stacey told William that on Monday the family would be coming with her to a lady who would help them talk about things. They would also be making a "family guide" that would help the whole family with the way each person acted with one another so there could be more fun and less arguing in the house. William came out from his pillow and smooshed his face into his mom's tummy. He breathed hard and then squeezed her arm. She squeezed back. Then he squeezed again. Then she squeezed back again! He giggled. Stacey had not heard him giggle in a long time.

Make Guidelines that Hold Children and their Parents Accountable

The next session with Stacey's whole family went well. We came up with a "family guide" and consequences and some rewards to look forward to if they were able to follow through with its guidelines, such as a cookout in the backyard that the kids chose the menu for and a special night of camping out in the living room with blanket forts, flashlights, and stories.

We made it known what is and is not acceptable in their family and what the consequences of poor choices were *ahead of time*. We made sure that Stacey and her husband were also held accountable. If parents do not listen to the guidelines, why would we expect that children would want to listen either? Honesty and authenticity are key. Highly sensitive children instinctively know when anybody is lying or being manipulative with them.

Months later, when Stacey was walking upstairs with me to my office, she stopped me. She was a little teary but managed to say,

> *Last week was Thanksgiving, you know. William actually ate some turkey. In the past, there would have been a meltdown long before dinner even got put on the table. I also want you to know that all four of us actually played Dogopoly. We have never played a board game all together as a family. This was the best Thanksgiving I have ever had. Thank you.*

I nodded in response since I knew nothing more needed to be said.

A Single Dad and his Daughter

It is almost always possible for parents to be able to guide their children to the desired behaviors if "front loading" and setting up win/win situations is used instead of waiting for situations to escalate and then trouble shooting when it is already too late. Most bad parenting happens in the heat of a situation once the situation is already heading downhill and starting to snowball.

Steve is a single parent with a highly sensitive four-year-old daughter. Gillian's sensitivities were mostly triggered when she was tired and also in noisy, crowded places. She was especially sensitive to fluorescent lighting and perfumes. On a Wednesday evening, Steve was running late at his office and did not have time to stop at the grocery store for dinner ingredients. Gillian had ballet that afternoon and was tired from a poor night's sleep the night before. She had finished ballet and was waiting for her dad to pick her up.

Unfortunately, Steve did not think ahead about what would have made the rest of the evening go smoothly. He also forgot that Gillian was on overload already from her lack of sleep. When Gillian got in the car, Steve was already rushed, harried, and running late. His own gas tank was on empty and had no energy to give his daughter. He was short tempered and crabby with his coworkers during the day. He told Gillian in a stern and loud voice to get in the car quickly because they had to get some dinner stuff at the market. Steve did not really consider the fact that the supermarket was probably the worst place they could have gone right then. His tone with Gillian was curt and impatient. And, because he was feeling so rushed, he did not ask her how ballet and their dress rehearsal went for her upcoming recital. I am sure you can probably see where this situation was heading: a full-blown meltdown in the supermarket checkout line and barely making it out of the store with groceries. Both of them were spent, and Gillian ended up just going to her room once they got home, not eating and staying to herself most of the rest of the night. Not only did dad dine alone, but he hardly needed to make the stop at the grocery store if Gillian was too sullen to eat anyhow. Actually, Steve was lucky that Gillian was an isolator when she was hurt and sad.

Steve's daughter tends to be internal, but many other parents deal with children that scream, bang their heads on walls, stomp, hit things and people, and throw things when this kind of situation happens. I see many children in my practice that break furniture and doors, throw remote controls, climb on tables, and punch their parents. Many parents report being verbally harassed in the car or their child kicking the back of the seat when they are driving. Some parents admit to me that they have hit back or hurt their children when trying to get them to sit in a "time out."

So how do we avoid these kinds of behaviors and ineffective consequences? How could things have gone differently?

For starters, Steve could have realized that he needed to refuel his own tank before he picked his daughter up so that his own tone and manner toward her was more welcoming, or at least neutral.

Highly Sensitive Children Pick up On Your Moods

Steve's daughter was already having a hard day and really needed support instead of a dad who was short with her. If Steve had taken the time to de-stress himself, he would have better been able to be available for his daughter. She probably really needed a big hug, welcoming tone, and perhaps to talk about how hard it was to get through ballet when she was so tired. She probably also needed some good old-fashioned TLC. If they had arrived at the supermarket after he talked to her a bit, instead of rushing, there would have been a different outcome. She was already on empty and then sank lower once her sensitive emotional system was affected by her dad's stress and anxiety. He also could have "front loaded" the situation beforehand for success.

Set the Tone and Boundaries of a Situation Beforehand

Steve could have taken some time to gather himself before he picked up Gillian so that the tone of the conversation had been welcoming and friendly:

> *Gillian, I know how tired you are today since you did not sleep well last night. I am feeling a little low on energy myself, but we really don't have much in the way of groceries at home, and I wanted to make us a good dinner. Do you want to help me by picking out some things at our favorite grocery store and then napping on the way home, or would you rather we go to the quick mart and hurry things up even though there are fewer foods there that you like?*
>
> *I know we will make this easy by just concentrating on dinner food for tonight and then getting right out of the store. I can also get you a piece of fruit to hold you over 'till dinner is ready tonight. You can think about what you want to choose until we get to the traffic light next to the church.*

By giving Gillian a choice, setting up the time limit in the store, and providing a treat for her in advance, she has more power and freedom. She will not feel like she is being dragged somewhere without choice and without knowing how long it will take. This will provide more safety and less stress for her since supermarkets are already a challenge for her light and crowd sensitivity. She will also feel taken into account and respected once her dad acknowledges her own needs. And since her dad would have already connected with her about her day, she would feel him present with her instead of her system feeling more stressed meeting a rushed and anxious father. The connection she has with him as they go into the store will be grounding for her, and provide her with more balance while she handles the things that trigger her own sensitivities. If they were holding hands or even having a little fun as they entered the store, she would be far less aware of how much the people and lighting are uncomfortable for her. She would have also felt like her dad was on her side in helping her handle the situation, not just dragging her through it.

And, of course, Steve could have taken a step back and decided to abort the whole mission and order something to be delivered to the house. Even though he felt anxious about being short on money that week, he may have wanted to put their emotional needs above their financial ones. It may have just been better to not push and just let the whole mission go. Is this one situation worth all the hassle? Maybe a bath, nap, bike ride, or snack at home would have just de-escalated the stressful day much better.

Have a Kid Comfort Care Kit in your Car

Since I frequently travel and know that I have many sensitivities that can be cumbersome on the road, I take special care to make sure I have some "emergency" tools that can help to balance me when things get overwhelming. I choose a car that is very comfortable and basic on the inside with fewer computerized bells, whistles, and gadgets, and it has "teddy bear" neutral colors that are easier on my system. I also have enough room in it to carry a large bin that has my emergency essentials: warm blanket, eye pillow, yoga cushion and extra snack are always in a bin in the back. There is also an extra sweatshirt and sneakers should I have a messy day or be really uncomfortable in something I chose to wear. I also keep one favorite meditation book, a pen, pad, scarf and lavender essential oil. There are always good CDs to listen to because I rarely turn on the radio due to all the commercials and bad news. But all these things *stay in the bin* so that they are easy to find, and I never have to think about it. What I take out of the bin goes back into the bin before I go back into my house. Otherwise, I am always searching for it.

I suggest this kind of "first-aid comfort kit" for a parent to keep in their car for their highly sensitive child.

Ideas for a comfort kit could include a blanket, extra sweater, earphones with good soothing music, eye pillow or hat to block out visual stimulation, an essential oil, some kind of good snack, a sketch pad with magic markers, and a favorite book that can be read more than once. Pass up on all the other electronics that seem to help in the short run, but in the longer run will actually drain your child even more. Depending on the age of your child, you could have one specific stuffed animal that is her "car buddy" that can keep her comfortable in the car. Do not bring this special stuffed animal in the house. If you keep it in the bin, it will maintain its "specialness" and soothing abilities and not become just one more thing that gets lost in the shuffle of a busy day.

Encourage your child to tell you when he feels he needs

something from the kit. Help him figure out the best solution for that moment. After you do this for a while, you will see that your child will learn what he needs on an ongoing basis for comfort and self care. Some questions to ask early on before a possible meltdown:

> *Are you tired, do you want the blanket?*
> *Do you have a headache that could be helped by the eye pillow or your hat?*
> *Is there so much noise that your earplugs would be helpful?*
> *Are your socks and shoes wet from the rain? Could you use the sneakers we have back there?*

Once you and your child get the hang of knowing what will help the discomfort, it becomes easier and more a part of your lifestyle. Self care is an art and needs to be practiced by the parent so the child can model this behavior. If a parent is always frustrated, irritated, curt, hungry, or tired, a child grows up thinking that self care may not be important. But if you verbalize and model ways that you care for yourself and set boundaries around these things, then your child will, too.

Rather than screaming above your children to "get them" to be more quiet in the car, make it a practice of just pulling over when the noise level is too high or the kids are acting out. Pull over, shut the car off, and just sit for a second. You will be surprised how fast the car will get quiet. Your children will want to know what is going on and they will look toward you to find that out, rather than you standing on your head shouting for them to pay attention to you.

Once you have their attention, turn around in your seat and calmly but forcefully say:

> *You know, I get headaches when things are too loud. And I have one right now. I can't drive if this continues. So, unless you all change your tone, we will just keep stopping the car and we will wait. If you want to be on time like the other kids in your dance class, then make some better choices and we can get going again.*

In general it is best to keep in mind that trying to get children's attention by yelling or screaming above them does not work well. It is much more advantageous to put your hand on their shoulders, to whisper, to turn off a light, to stop your car or do something less predictable than nag, yell, or say their names a hundred times. Also, remember that you do not make a request and then say, "Okay?" in a questioning tone. You are not asking them a question for them to say yes or no to. You are stating a request that you expect them to follow. The question tone at the tail end of your sentence invalidates what it is that you are communicating to them. You would be surprised how many parents do not even know they are doing this.

Your child will know whether you mean business by your inner power and authenticity. If you give her the chance to refuse your request by giving her the choice to do so, she will almost always choose to have a power struggle with you to test your boundaries. Keep lovingly firm. Do not skimp on this rule of thumb. You will be sorry later on. Take the time to enforce these habits consistently. It will make your job easier in the long run.

Chapter 10

The Spiritual World of the Intuitive Child

I walked into their home to meet Amy, a seven-year-old who lived with her mom and sister in their condo. Amy's mom took one of my classes at an expo and wanted me to meet her daughter to confirm what she really already knew. Her daughter was what I would call a classic Indigo without the hyperactivity or imbalances that some other Indigos suffer from. Her mom had known that this girl was special from the moment of inception when she would send messages to her pregnant mother telepathically. The child practically told her mother what she wanted to be named. This mother was well along a spiritual path, and because she was not scared by her daughter's spiritual gifts, they continued to bloom throughout their time together both in vitro and in life.

When I entered the living room and we set eyes on each other, it was magnetic.

"Hey I remember you! We were in Egypt together. Sorry that wasn't such a great time for you," she said compassionately. "I bet it will be better this time that you are the grown up and I am the kid." I laughed knowing full well that what she said was true. I was staring at a bright-eyed six-year-old healer who was beaming with light.

"I can see your aura, and it's real pretty, just like you." I blushed, but immediately felt at home with her. She felt the same way.

I pulled out my art box and placed it on the kitchen table. We drew quietly together at first, and then she said, "Here are the fairies I can see in my room with green and blue wings; they look like Christmas lights. Sometimes they have wings, and sometimes not, but they love my bedroom. I build them places to sleep and hang out in my room. They visit quite often."

She loved to draw fairies and angels and write poems about them—each one with a different name and distinct in its character. "I love my angels, but my fairy friends are even more fun. They love playing like I do." Then she smiled and asked if we could add watercolor to our pastel drawings.

Many of the children I work with are not as lucky to have such acceptance and confidence in the spiritual gifts they possess, and many come from homes that do not honor the kinds of gifts that they have. This is one of the reasons why so many of these children lose touch with their unique spiritual connection. Some of the most common gifts of a spiritually sensitive child are:

❖ Seeing colors or the aura around a person or animal
❖ Sensing or seeing angels or deceased loved ones they may or may not have known before
❖ Having strong intuition, psychic abilities, and hunches that are right on the mark
❖ Sensing the energy of another person, picking up other people's energy
❖ Strong connection to crystals, fairies, dolphins, unicorns, or mermaids
❖ Can communicate easier with animals than people, and sometimes prefers it
❖ Strong social justice connection, wants to save the world and other people that she may not even know
❖ Wise and knows spiritual techniques or hands-on healing protocols that he has not studied; he just knows it
❖ Artistic, musical, scientific, or theatrical gifts beyond her years

These children have gifts in an arena that is unfamiliar and sometimes shunned by the society we live in. Our society believes in and values academic giftedness, but what about social, emotional, or spiritual giftedness? Do these abilities count as ones to be honored and encouraged?

When a spiritually gifted child spends eight hours a day in a place that does not acknowledge or honor who he really is and where his gifts lay, when does he get to shine? This lack of affirmation is particularly exacerbated if he is born into a family that does not believe in these kinds of gifts anyway. So into hiding it all goes. Or even worse, unattended to, it creates feelings of shame, uniqueness, and isolation. This all leads to The Big Three: anger, depression, and anxiety.

If the child does not have an ally and an outlet for her gifts and passions, slowly over the elementary school years, these unique talents just fade away or are shamed away by people who cannot understand them. In the same way that adults need to have this part of their lives validated and enriched, children do too. What the intuitive or spiritually gifted child needs is a role model or mentor who can help to validate feelings, boost self-esteem, encourage connection, and promote self-acceptance. We need to make spiritual giftedness a priority in the same way that we have made academic giftedness one. In reality, it is only our society that has its priorities skewed, not these children's. They have it right. We have to be reminded what is of the greatest need at this time in our world. Would it not make more sense to put social and emotional learning to the *top* of the priority list for our families and our schools?

We can start by doing this at home. It is helpful to start affirming your child's spiritual and emotional experience when he is young. It is best to find a caring and non-judgmental way to have open communication about it. You can be creative with the kind of wording you use and try to make how you talk about it commonplace and part of what is accepted at home. You may share your own personal experiences honestly, but do not push. Your child will know when it is safe to share his experiences with you. Sometimes seeking out a spiritual counselor, aunt, or uncle may help, since your child may be too self-conscious to share with you. Encouraging him to write in a journal is also a way of having him affirm his own experience. The more you can do to help your child know that his worldview is important and valued, the better. Children are also our spiritual teachers who have agreed to come and remind us about what is really important. Let us hear them and take action upon their message to us. They are here to recalibrate the global compass and the direction it needs to point toward.

Tips & Tools for Your Child's Spirit

✧ Take your child to a health-food store, wellness center, or metaphysical store where she can pick out some crystals, books, or bedtime music. Your child will almost always know what is best for her body and spirit.

✧ Make a game out of his psychic gifts such as "I wonder if..." where you guess who is calling on the phone before you pick it up, or how many email messages he has before he looks, or who is at the door. Have fun with your intuitive side.

✧ Set intentions or goals together before the day starts and visualize positive outcomes happening effortlessly.

✧ Have fun doing a collage of goals or things she wants to bring into her life. Use visualization with magazine clippings.

✧ Purchase books on mermaids, unicorns, dolphins, fairies, animals, and angels.

✧ Enroll him in a spiritual class, even if it is for adults.

✧ Purchase The Kids Yoga Deck and do yoga at home together or go to yoga class. Have big yoga balls around your house to exercise and play on.

✧ Be present to your child and her inner child. If she sees that you honor her and your own inner child, she will know it is important for her to be a kid and not a "wise old soul" all the time. She needs play and silliness too.

✧ Look for and capitalize on "teachable moments" that

can help exemplify the principles of spiritual living that are important in your household.

✧ Hold your child often; send him positive energy and thoughts of comfort instead of trying to manage his life. Trust that he will be taken care of even if your child seems "different" than other children.

✧ Make wonder, adventure, and exploration part of everyday living in your household. Remember that the 9-5 world and school systems are man-made constructs.

✧ Practice generosity and abundance with your child by modeling ways she can give to the world. Pick a cause to support that you both care about to give your time, attention, or money to. Practice manifesting things with wishes, pictures, collages, and verbal requests. Celebrate when things come forth effortlessly.

✧ Encourage your child to trust his guidance, gut, and hunches. Point out when he has success in following his inner guidance in small and big ways in his life.

✧ Spend time in silence, nature, and just being with no schedule, agenda, or time constraints.

✧ Get in the car without a map and ask to be guided to something fun. Then let your inner voice tell you which way to turn and follow the guidance. Go where this takes you.

✧ Encourage your child to bond with animals, be in nature as much as possible, and practice healing techniques on you. Let her know when you feel something physically. See if she can pick up on the problem and help heal it with her hands through Reiki, positive energy, or affirmations.

Chapter 11

The Family System: What We Can Learn from the Dolphins

Although human beings consider themselves to be the most evolved species, they have much to learn about the meaning of family and community. In today's day and age, we often live isolated lives from each other and the larger community around us. It is sometimes so dangerous in our streets that we are afraid to let our children play alone in our neighborhoods, and our kids are so booked up with soccer games and lessons that there is hardly time left for free play or dinner together. Many children have two parents who must work full time, which makes quality time together fall by the wayside. If a family is fortunate enough to have weekends together, it is usually spent doing errands or shopping at the mall, with little time for play, touch, talking, or listening. Our fast-paced culture has forgotten what is important: time spent with each other. Of course, there are families that are quite lucky to escape this American phenomenon, but much can be learned if we consider what dolphins know as a species.

Dolphins live and travel in pods that are bonded together. They are interdependent on one another, and this is seen as one of the highest values in dolphin society. Dolphins are almost always seen in groups of two or more, and they interact closely with their families, often touching or holding fins as they swim and travel. Dolphins that swim together will often consciously synchronize their breathing as they glide through the water for extended periods of time. In addition, they regularly gaze at one another and closely coordinate their movements in unison. Most dolphins will start their day with a ritual of circling with one another for an hour or so before anything else is done. In addition to this group bonding process, they play, jump, dive, communicate, sing, stroke, breathe, baby-tend, grieve, birth, and eat as a group.

Dolphins actually live the saying "family first" and stick together as an extended family and pod from birth to death. In fact, family bonds are so strong that if members of a pod become trapped in fishing nets, the whole pod stays together until all the dolphins are free. Similarly, if a baby dolphin becomes trapped, his mother will attempt to enter the net in order to die with him. Mass stranding of dolphins are thought by some people to be an entire pod following a few sick or stranded pod members to their death. Dolphins will often carry their sick with them for days at a time without stopping, until assistance is no longer required. Telepathic communication is one of the preferred means of communication for cetacean ocean animals, yet we think that speech is the highest form of communication and place a very high importance on when a child first speaks out loud. Many late-blooming speakers are actually using telepathy as their primary form of communication, as we have learned with the highly sensitive children and many autistic children too. This is why dolphins bond so easily with autistic children, Indigos, and crystal children; they speak the same language. Their energetic vibrations match one another, and telepathy or music is the preferred language. Love and touch is of the highest priority, along with discipline and boundaries. To establish discipline and boundaries with their young as well as with others, wild dolphins use posturing gestures such as tail slapping, tooth-raking, or face-to-face head nodding. This is very interesting, since dolphins are among the world's strongest animals and are able to dominate or kill sharks if necessary. Dolphins rarely use their power and strength to kill or cause disharmony among them or other species. They rarely use their power in violent or aggressive ways. In contrast to some of the physical discipline we sometimes see in our family culture, dolphins and whales hold crisply and firmly to their boundaries without violence or physical punishment.

If there is one parenting issue I see over and over again with the families I work with, it is the issue of boundaries. Since Indigo and highly sensitive children have iron-clad wills and often complain about boundaries if not given what they want when they want it, many parents cave in to avoid the trouble and the energy it takes to get through the unpleasantries of sticking to a boundary. But the thing these children need the most is firm and lovingly set boundaries that are consistent, even though they will do just about anything to avoid them. It is the way we enact the boundaries that can either make them effective or ineffective.

Boundaries and Limits are Important

Your child will need to know what the expectations and guidelines are in a clear and consistent manner up front. I often help families come up with a contract or credo that we make together with the whole family that outlines and states what the family guidelines are for the children and the adults. Each member of the family gets to have their say, and there can be negotiating, but once the guidelines are drawn up and signed, that's it! All parties have agreed on what is appropriate and allowed. If screaming is something that they hate (and of course they usually do), then even the adults have to monitor their own behavior and make apologies or restitution if a slip up happens. So know what your limits are and what the consequences are for family members if those limits are not adhered to. Be specific. Be clear. Live up to your part of the agreement as well.

Let your kids come up with ideas for their own consequences. Usually, they will come up with something far more meaningful if given the chance. Enforce the consequence with as little emotionality, repetition, and screaming as possible. Let your child know what they did and how you feel about the behavior, not them. Tell them how inappropriate the behavior is, not how bad they are for doing it. If they could do it better, they would. There is usually an underlying feeling-based reason a child misbehaves or makes a poor choice. Try to stand back and see what the underlying need is.

Do they need affection? Play? Connection? Sleep? Your time? Are they overloaded, under-stimulated, sad, or lonely? Have you promised something that you didn't deliver? Have you been short with them, upset, or impatient? Has their school day been hard due to non-activity, boredom, challenging material, or too much non-nutritious cafeteria food? Be a detective. Always look for the need that lies beneath the undesired behavior and see if there is a way to meet that need.

If screaming at and nagging children were really effective, we would have very well-behaved children by now in our society. We need to be more creative and wise about the way we teach discipline to our kids. The more you repeat and say things over and over, the less effective you become as their parent. Indigos never respond well to meaningless rules and the old style of parenting we received as kids. Many parents I work with are afraid they will be viewed as ineffective parents if they do not protect, warn, and be authoritarian with their children. We need to take the risk of parenting in a new way to be effective with these children. Know that you only need answer to your own conscience, and it will be scary the first time you allow your kid to not take a coat because she says she is not cold, or fail a class because he says it is meaningless learning for him. She will not die from the cold, and maybe school is meaningless for him because he needs something else like art lessons, a marine biology program, or to start working on his life purpose in a vocational school. Maybe failing at something because he did not study will be a better deterrent than you being his homework enforcer.

Remember to note and compliment your child when she is doing the right thing. Be specific about what exactly she is doing that is helpful or positive to you. Tell her how much you love her often, and not just at the end of a controversy. Send love letters in lunch boxes, and put sticky notes on mirrors.

When you see that the temperature of a situation is rising, ask that your child take a break, cool-off period, or time out. Then come back to the situation, clearly stating your limits and offering a choice to her. If your child refuses to take a cool-off period or continues on, then you have every right to remove yourself from the situation and go for your own cool-off period.

An example of offering choices would be:

> *It is really not okay that you carry on like this in the store because you want candy. You know what our rule is about sugar, and I am sorry that you are feeling angry about that rule. But your choices are to leave the store with Daddy and take a walk outside, or choose a treat from the kinds of foods you know are good choices for your body such as pretzel sticks or yogurt popsicle. So which would you prefer?*

Then stop. Do not repeat a thousand times. Do not bend your boundary. Do not shout. If your child feels you will cave in and cater to his desire, ultimately, he will not feel that you are the adult who will take care of him and hold the container for him, and he will disrespect or try to manipulate you in the future. It is best to get the hard work out of the way first. If you are overly emotional, then you may need more time out too. Take it, and then return to the situation. The more escalated your child is, the more calm you need to become to offset his reactivity.

Try to explain the reasoning for your boundaries as much as you can. The more your child understands your reasoning, the less she will feel powerless and under random authority regulations. It is best to use "I" statements and tell your child what you are feeling in the moment. Believe me, they can feel it anyway, so you might as well be authentic and upfront. These children need authenticity and explanation whenever it is possible. These ways of phrasing it that can work well:

> *You know, when you are screaming like this I feel really scared and it even hurts my ears. I wish you could tell me what you need instead of yelling. I really want to help you and see how we can work this out. It is hard to feel so frustrated, so how can I help you?*
>
> *I know you hate standing in line and it is hard for you to be patient. I have a hard time waiting also, but I know I would feel angry of someone on line in back of us all of the sudden budged in front of us in line. So how about we play I spy and see how many minutes it really takes for us to get to the checkout? I bet it is less than four minutes; what's your guess?*

If all else fails and you can't come up with a logical reason for something, I find this one usually works and is funny too:

> *Well, on the planet you come from they may not have to wait ever, but here on Earth we gotta do it the way other Earthlings do. (Then smile.)*

If you know you are going into a situation that is hard, prepare your child first for it by talking with them about how he feels, maybe rehearsing possible outcomes, and offering a reward or treat if he can act appropriately. Try to use something that is not food and will be win/win, like time spent alone with mom, a special treat at the art store, or points toward a larger reward like new sneakers or something that will help him with his passions. Verbalize the specific ways your child has done well; don't just say "good job." Tell him you really liked the way he was able to wait for the two hours while you had your doctor appointment and what a great choice he made by reading and drawing while he sat and waited. Keep a jar of earned marbles or pennies that is added up towards something larger at a later date. This helps him to learn how to work for something that is not immediately gratified.

Fun and acceptance are what make kids want to be around adults. Remember how much time and play the dolphins do together? When people are having fun and feeling connected, they usually forget to make poor choices or argue about everything. The more you can concentrate on the positive qualities of your Indigo and build on those, the better. Yes, these children challenge us, our old parenting paradigms, and can really push our buttons. But our souls made the choice to be their guides (or be guided by them), so remember this fact. We are meant to learn from these wise beings and listen to them, but we are still meant to parent them. We cannot allow them to rule the house, be our best friend, have their way always, or become entitled in everything they do. If they know you are at their mercy, they will not respect you and the situation will feel unsafe for them. When children do not feel safe, they act out and push the behavioral envelope. When they argue or are sticking to their point of view, they need to be given ample time to talk about their point of view and feelings in a situation. Take the time to do this. It is time well spent even if inconvenient at times. After this is finished, stick to the limits that you have set forth. It will be hard at first, but you will see that your children will come to trust you more and more, and then may even surprise you by making good choices for themselves even when you are not present.

Many teens will make what we consider poor choices later on down the road. If this happens, it is usually best to let them live out the consequences of these choices. Their experiences will be their best teacher, and we should not protect them from everything. Ask that their angels protect them and then get on with your own life. You may have anxiety that will really kick in. Call your support network, your sister, your therapist, your angels, but do not keep calling your teen. It will push her farther away. Practice letting go for your sake and hers. Her experiences are for her to learn from, even if they may seem "negative" to you. If you allow her appropriate freedoms, she will eventually come back to you of her own free will and will appreciate the space you have given her as a gift. We do not own our children; they are on loan to us so we can help prepare them for adulthood.

Time in Connection

If boundaries are the most prevalent issue I see affecting families, then time together would be second. We have become a culture that has fenced in our yards and families and fenced out the connection to each other and the larger community around us. It is rare to see kids able to just go out and see who is on the block to play with, and since fewer children are out there, they retreat to the confines of their own homes with television and computer. We have created quite a mess for ourselves, and because we have to work so hard to live in "safe" places with great schools, we are never home to enjoy each other and the fruits of our labors. Fathers have sometimes had to become absent, and mothers are also being pulled in too many directions. Teachers at school and in after-school programs are spending more time with our own children than we are. Kids are forced into long days that are over stimulating and too long and then being told they have attentional issues. Maybe the "attention deficit" is in the amount of time they are really paid attention to in loving, caring, and connected ways. Maybe our society is creating people that are so overloaded that we cannot attend to any one thing at a time properly. If we are constantly on the move and being encouraged to pick up our pace in all areas of our lives with technology, over scheduling, and too many competing responsibilities, is it possible to give the people and details in our lives the attention that is warranted?

We have to start getting out of the fast-paced rat race and really attend to what is important. Our priorities have shifted so much from self and family preservation that we have forgotten what really needs attending to and first priority. So how do we make the shift back? The first key is to become aware. Notice how much of your family's week is spent connecting together. Do you actually have conversations at your dinner table, or are you all rushing from or to somewhere else? Pay attention to each other and what you do together. If hard work or long hours have to take priority, then can you at least start with a solid block of time that is consistently set aside each week for each child? Just as married couples are starting to have "date nights" so they can spend quality time together, families need time together to play, connect, and have time to relax.

One great way to connect is to play high point/low point at the dinner table. Each family member gets time to be heard and listened to while he or she talks about the best part of the day and the most challenging part of the day. Adults are included in this. Ask questions when the person is done. See if you can brainstorm around difficult issues that come up or offer comfort and support just by being present. Most children want your attention, not your opinions. If you proactively give them the time and care they are craving, they will not have to seek out negative behaviors to get your attention. The attention will already be on them. Fill your cup first by having some time to yourself during the week so you can be present to them. Solve marital difficulties at another time and place. Meals should be enjoyable and positive so families want to be together. If dinner together most nights is not possible, then start out with one or two nights a week. If you cannot do this because of job responsibilities or financial obligations, consider changing the family lifestyle by moving to a less-expensive area, renting instead of owning a home, or spending vacation time at home instead of going to exotic places. Most families get overwhelmed by all the things they have to do on a vacation anyway, and then they end up stressed out. Do fun day trips in the car or go on a nature walk. Everyone will feel less stressed, and you may even end up enjoying time together more.

Try doing less and "being" more. One or two days a week with after-school activities and sports is really adequate. Kids today are so overbooked with their schedules and lessons that they hardly know what it is like to just take an afternoon bike ride after school or sit by a tree and see leaves fall.

If we want our kids to be able to attend to life, we must teach them how to attend to themselves by slowing down and taking in the world around them. Their senses need to be touched by things that are real and rich in flavor, texture, color, and tactility. When they are indoors with no movement and man-made technology, they lose their connection to that which nourishes them. Obviously, we cannot give our children what we do not have ourselves, so it behooves us to live in ways that are more wholesome and sustaining ourselves. If we create a safe and loving container for them to come home to, we will see that they can grow hearty with strong roots. It is these roots that are needed in our society to ensure that our children have the foundation from which to make healthy choices for themselves and become resilient in facing the challenges they will ultimately need to overcome. If they learn to do this in their family of origin, then they can pass this legacy on to the family they may start on their own some day.

Tips & Tools for Family Life

✧ Keep a job jar or use a spin wheel to determine who does which chores. There will be less fighting and it can even be fun.

✧ Use the "seesaw" technique. When your child's emotions escalate, your emotions should get calmer instead of being triggered by hers.

✧ Make a gratitude list at the dinner table and add pictures if you have artistic-minded kids. Hang it up on the refrigerator.

✧ Process your own feelings and issues with an adult so that they do not affect your children.

✧ Ask more questions than give answers. Listen.

✧ Remember that "No," is actually a complete sentence. When you stick to your "No"s, then your child respects your boundary and trusts that you cannot be manipulated. This feels safe to him even if he tries to act out.

✧ Remember that people are more important than things or schedules. Do half of what you think you must do in a day and give that time to yourself or your kids.

✧ Use "I" statements such as, "When I had just finished cleaning everything and then it was all messed up five minutes later, I felt really frustrated. I need for you to clean up the mess that you left behind yourself."

✧ Give as much choice is possible within every situation. This enables your child to feel power in ways that are healthy.

✧ Remind yourself that for whatever reasons, you and your child picked each other to learn with and from in this lifetime. Try to see the grand scheme at work rather than just the daily annoyances or hardships. Life is short; don't wait to really appreciate the ones you are with.

✧ Have a board game night once a week. Spend a night with no electricity, technology, and camp out even if you use tents in the living room. Remember flashlights and forts?

✧ Frame things in the positive instead of the negative. Say things like, "In our house we solve things with feeling words and respectful language," instead of, "No hitting or cursing!"

✧ Have family meetings where each member of the family can state what he or she needs or wants from other family members or needs in general. Do whatever you can to support these needs and wants appropriately and within reason.

✧ Model how amends are made when you miss the mark so your children will also know how to take responsibility for their actions and apologize when necessary. Showing your children your humanness is a great gift you can do for them.

✧ Look for ways that your family can connect and help the community around you. Children need a way to be of service and connected to the larger world around them in order to have better perspective and appreciate what they have.

Chapter 12

Adult Indigos
Coming out of the Closet

Surprisingly enough, after I appeared on A&E Network as a therapist working with psychic children, I did not get bombarded with calls from parents with Indigo children who needed support. Instead, I received many emails and calls from all over the country from *adults* who wanted to tell someone that they had gifts as a child that were shamed or invalidated. They wanted to come out of the closet to someone who understood. They wanted to reclaim the gifts they had pushed away or found too hard to manage peacefully as a child and now an adult. The following is a list that I have seen most prevalent in these adults:

❖ Some sensitivities similar to the children described in this book
❖ Trouble establishing boundaries in relationships, chronic

care takers, burned-out professional helpers, taking on feelings of others, weight problems

❖ Rapid heart palpitations, ringing in the ear, trouble sleeping

❖ Scattered attention span, difficulty completing creative projects and ideas, problems surviving in the workplace due to atmosphere, difficulty getting along with boss or coworkers

❖ Depression, suicidal thoughts, wanting to go "home"

❖ Trouble integrating spiritual beliefs into a grounded practical way in the world that works emotionally and financially

❖ Outgrowing marital partners and friends because of differences in goals in the world and world outlook

❖ Physical discomfort in the body including feet, knees, lower back, and shoulders

❖ Outgrowing religious institutions that used to bring some degree of comfort and learning

❖ Wanting to get off, slow down, or jump off this planet

❖ Challenges managing anger, emotions, grounding energy, and will seek out carbohydrate foods to do this if necessary

❖ Needing biochemical help such as antidepressants, homeopathy, light therapy, living by water, living in a sunny place, or any endorphin-helping activity to help stabilize low mood, low energy, or irritability

❖ Needing to rest or nap more often during the day, needing to retreat from the world, traffic, and be in a low sensory or even dimly lit place

❖ Rejection of the 9-5 world and the American Dream, doing things on a different timeline and for different, more meaningful reasons, yet still trying to find some way to live effectively and purposefully

❖ Experienced abuse, addiction, or shame in family of origin and/or religion of origin; usually the "black sheep" in the family system; using spiritual family, 12-step group, community, or marital partner as "family of choice" or support network

❖ Had psychic, intuitive, clairvoyant, or inexplicable spiritual experiences as a child that were not talked about or shamed

❖ Had near-death experience as a child or accident prone—including broken bones, multiple car accidents. and reckless adventures—as a child or adult

❖ Have undiagnosed dyslexia or been labeled ADD, OCD, or bipolar as a child or adult

❖ Gave birth to Indigo, crystal, autistic, or learning disabled child who share many of their characteristics

❖ Prefer to be earning a living pursuing passions and not working to earn a living in more traditional ways

❖ Experiencing rapid manifestation of desires on the material plane when at one's best, negative thoughts come to fruition rather quickly if not monitored

❖ Not having the same relationship with time that one used to, feeling scattered much of the time

❖ Finding that just raising children is about all that one can handle; wanting to shake up, break up, or pull one's children out of the school they are in; considering home

schooling, Waldorf, or trade school for one's child to
help both parent and child survive

Many adults who I work with confess to me that they too
had hid their experiences from the world so they could survive
in their families, schools, or religious communities. Most are
now highly sensitive adults who either found it too hard to
function in the world and had retreated from it, are healers who
had survived but have no idea how to incorporate their gifts
into the real world and make money, or are 20-somethings that
are now depressed, smoking cigarettes or pot to numb their
bodies, and feel suicidal at times. They all wondered the same
thing. "Are there Indigo adults? I know I am older than these
kids, but that describes me to a T."

The answer is yes. Call it whatever you want to: highly
sensitive, Indigo, ADD, artistically gifted, intuitively gifted,
psychic, light worker, or healer. The truth is that all these labels
are describing the same thing; the evolution of the human
spirit as we become more evolved as a species and learn that
we are spiritual beings having a human experience, not human
beings trying to "get" spiritual. Some of us are just further
along this path than others. And the ones leading the way are
usually the most confused because they are the trailblazers for
the rest. Soon it may be more the norm to know how to be
our own best spiritual advisor, channel information from our
own deceased loved ones and angels, know what others are
thinking instinctively, and stay connected to our truth always,
not just when we are able to. This will be the thing that will
transform the atrocities of today's society that need our help.
These children we call "Indigo" are just more fully actualized

at a younger age, and because of this, we are more willing to listen; both because we are surprised and stunned into belief, and also because we are more desperate than we ever have been.

Things are coming to a head with the dark getting so dark, but the light getting so much more apparent. We know this in our souls, but we can't quite grasp it and hold onto it as truth yet all the time. We have fleeting remembering moments that are cherished and yearned for. If only we could stay in that remembering and connected place more often we would feel so much better. Well, we can. We are just being called to stand up in our truth and do the footwork. The more we do this for ourselves, the more we can get on board with the kids who are driving the bus we need to be on. We are continually stunned that the bus driver could be so young! How could they know? Let's not let these young prophets and unbelievably wise souls go unnoticed, unheard, overmedicated, or shamed in their giftedness. Let's own our inner power and in so doing, we can validate theirs too. We can do this. We came here to be a part of this miracle in one way or another. Let us be the miracle we want so desperately to believe in. The world needs the sensitivity and depth that these children and teens have to offer. If we honor these qualities and create a world that supports these children, we will see that the world will become a more humane, compassionate, and sensitive place. We are all in need of this now. May we see it happen in our lifetime.

Epilogue: The "Me" Instant Gratification Nation: How Society Helps to Create ADHD

A box of Crayola crayons, hopscotch, looking out the window of a car, tinker toys, and tea cups. I wonder if children in the year 2015 will even know what these things are. Will they sit under a tree watching a leaf slowly dance from its branch? Have time to ever just to sit and wonder? A day without a cell phone? Or Saturday that is not scheduled with five things too many?

I walked into CVS to get Tylenol, Advil, or anything that would help the horrid headache and stuffiness in my nose and chest. I made my way up to the pharmacy register with my Advil and was greeted by the white lab coated attendant at the register.

He looked at me and asked, "Cold or allergies?" as he punched in $3.29.

"Oh, allergies," I said.

"Oh, good."

"What's so good about allergies?" I muttered.

"Oh, nothing," he said. "It's just that I can't get sick. I

already used one day last month and I don't have any sick days coming…blah blah blah, blah blah blah."

Something made me sad and then even miffed.

I thought he was asking about me, concerned that I was suffering. But I was just in the way of his thinking about himself, really. A product of the "me" generation. Me texting, me blogging, me twittering about my blog, me watching someone getting hurt and recording on my phone it so it can be sent to my 268 "friends" to ogle at. All done within seconds of the event even finishing its occurrence.

Me. Me. Me. Fast. Fast. Fast. Me.

What have we created in our society?

A parent emailed me today. Her daughter was in crisis and was regressing. The mother was in a panic, and wanted a phone consult set up right away.

I offered Monday or Wednesday. She said she works, and the kids all have soccer and they don't get home until eight o'clock. I offered Thursday, but cheerleading starts and the high school rehearsal does not let out until late. I emailed back saying that perhaps I could offer her one of my three open hours on Saturdays. That would never work because her husband is working overtime and both kids have double booked birthday parties, and they still had gifts to buy.

The next email took me by surprise. How about nine o'clock Tuesday evening or better yet, did I work on Sundays?

My heart sank. And, actually, I realized that in reality I knew what was probably going on with her daughter even without talking to the mother. They had forgotten to schedule love and time into their schedule. They did not realize that most children need time to think, time to rest, time to play in woods, and time to do nothing. They need time to draw with 1 of the 120 crayons in the box, to have a tea party with their favorite stuffed animal and blanket in the backyard, and to make forts in the woods.

It's the same old story. Kid can't sit still. School wants the parent to medicate. Kid sits and texts all day long and then is rushed to 100 errands after 40 different after school activities. No time to even stop back home to get the pink ballet slippers that were left by the door by the six-year-old. Is it ADHD, the parents all ask.

Yes, and we are creating it. Our very habits and patterns as a society are creating a problem that then we have to later fix.

Fast food. Fast track. Big curriculum. Longer days. Less time. Better scores. Have more, do more, and be more. And if a child cannot keep up with this pace or cannot perform, we allow ourselves to believe that maybe a new video game reward or a different psychotropic drug can be the answer.

We have become numb to each other, numb to the pain and isolation that our ways have caused and feel powerless to do anything about it. Running faster on the treadmill to keep up. And our children have suffered because of it. They have bared the brunt of our troubles. Attention deficit.

Who really has the deficit? Is it we who have become too busy to attend to each other and attend to the important but small details of life?

We must attend to our children who sometimes spend more time in school with their teachers than at home with parents. Attend to each other when we get allergies or sick and need a friendly support—even if from the CVS pharmacist. Attend to tea cups, crayons, sand castles, and things that are real. Attend to real friends—not the kind on Facebook that can be "unfriended" in an instant. Attend to each other at a meal without a spouse on the phone or daughter texting under the table. Attend to our own feelings and fears and tears that have no time to even come to the surface because we are distanced from ourselves, each other, and life.

Did you know that at a local elementary school, kindergarteners go to school five days a week, from 7:45 until 3:30?

Did you know that one parent at my lecture in Pittsburgh was called a child abuser by her doctor because she did not want to give her kid Ritalin? And one elementary school in New York has banned running at recess. The children are only allowed to skip since it is thought to be safer.

You should know these things and know that we must change our ways if we are going to change the patterns that are plaguing our children.

We need to get back to basics. Teacups and crayons matter.

CPSIA information can be obtained at www.ICGtesting.com
Printed in the USA
LVOW050117260613

340019LV00002B/112/P